Angela Stewart-Park, a designer and writer, and Jules Cassidy, an Australian writer, are both in their late twenties and live in East London. They met in 1974 in the Gateways Club, Chelsea, and since then have worked together on posters, articles and books for and about women.

WE'RE HERE
Conversations with lesbian women

Jules Cassidy and Angela Stewart-Park

Photographs by Angela Stewart-Park and J. P. Goodchild

QUARTET BOOKS   LONDON   MELBOURNE   NEW YORK

First published by Quartet Books Limited 1977
A member of the Namara Group
27 Goodge Street, London W1P 1FD

Copyright © 1977 by Jules Cassidy and Angela Stewart-Park

Photographs copyright © Angela Stewart-Park and Jules Cassidy

Typeset by Bedford Typesetters Limited

Printed in Great Britain by The Anchor Press Ltd
and bound by Wm Brendon & Son Ltd
both of Tiptree, Essex

ISBN 0 7043 3117 9

For J.P. (Joanie) Goodchild, Sally (Jaws) Bradberry,
Stephanie Dowrick, Rita Hambrook, Sylvia Room,
Sophie Esmond, Julia Langton, Janne Holmes, Val Evans,
Julie (Saj) Philips, Caroline Forbes and Sharon Nassauer, who
made this book with us.

CONTENTS

Introduction

This book is not trying to prove anything about lesbians, it's just to say, 'We're here.' Although it is about eleven specific lesbian women, in some ways it is about all of us. Many of the experiences you will read about are experiences many or most overt lesbians have had.

It's not just our book. We didn't write it on our own either. We couldn't have done it without endless help and support from other lesbians. It belongs to all lesbians. It was produced first for them. We hope many other people read it too, but it's for us first and foremost because we don't often get to read books that mention us at all, and when we do they present us as case-histories, not people; they try to justify us as 'normal' (we're certainly not normal in straight terminology, we have our own very distinct differences which we're proud of); or they're written purely to give a sex buzz at our expense. Thousands of books have been written about 'lesbians' by men, fantasies for male titillation. We feel that it is important that there should be one book somewhere that shows some ordinary lesbians to the world in an open and honest way. It doesn't say anything about lesbians in general. All that one can accurately say about lesbians in general is that they exist. No one can guess or estimate how many lesbians there are because so many of us are still in the closet.

When we come out of the closet – that is, admit publicly that we are lesbians – it's rather like out of the frying pan into the fire. None of us enjoys living in the closet. It implies first that we are ashamed of our sexuality; secondly, it isolates us from each other; and thirdly, it makes it difficult to have an honest relationship with anyone. Once we come out, we risk losing our jobs, our friends, the relationships we have with our families; and if we have children we risk losing them. Lesbians nearly always lose their children in custody cases.

All the women interviewed in this book are real women. These are their real names you are about to read, and their real photographs you are to look at. Some of them are risking a considerable amount by being so open about their sexuality.

Society doesn't like to give us any space to be ourselves openly because we are an alternative. We're an alternative to heterosexuality, which is projected as the norm. We question, just by being here, many values which are part of heterosexuality. We question monogamy. We question marriage. We question women's dependence on men. We question male/female role-playing. We question the sexuality of every human being who thinks they're normal.

What's so natural, normal and fulfilling about heterosexuality? Natural is what feels good, normal is feeling ordinary, fulfilled is when you just did what you felt like doing. Anyone can be any or all of these things, and no one except themselves can possibly know whether or not they are. What is it that makes heterosexuals feel so insecure about themselves that they can allow no alternative sexuality? How solid are the foundations upon which they build their moral values?

We two have been lovers for two and a half years. This book has come out of our relationship. We don't see lesbianism as purely a personal issue. It's a political issue for us and for all women. We've made a choice. We've chosen to relate to women sexually and emotionally. We've chosen not to relate to men in these ways. We feel that this choice has made us strong. Both of us have had relationships with men, both of us have loved and still do love some men. Both of us felt that heterosexuality drained our energy and did not allow us to develop as strong, independent individuals. We've worked through many different problems of relating together. We've fought over jealousy and monogamy and come out the other side. We've come to know that a strong relationship is not something that happens by magic with the one right person. It's something that happens after a lot of hard work, a lot of shared experience, a lot of laughter, a lot of tears, and endless, honest discussion. And when it's happened it doesn't magically stay all right without a lot more of the same.

Both of us are nearly thirty, both of us wasted a lot of years as isolated lesbians trying unsuccessfully to be straight. If the

Women's Movement had been as strong then, we could have found out a lot about ourselves and had the support of other women. If there had been one single book that showed us other lesbians and talked about them and us and about our sexuality, it would have made us feel less alone, less lonely.

We know that a woman does not need to have a man. We know that a child does not need to have a father. We know that no one needs to have the same lover for the rest of their life. We know we don't have to have an orgasm to enjoy making love. We know we don't have to make love unless we want to. We know our lovers because we know ourselves. We know that we can and will understand and control our own bodies. We know that we can talk to each other without speaking. We know that most of what we've been told about sex and about women is a tissue of lies. We know we're not freaks. We know we're beautiful, sensitive, sensual and womanly. We know that women have always loved women, and that we'll go on doing it for ever.

Pauline Willert
and Pauline Heap

Pauline Willert is twenty-eight. She was born in Gillingham, Kent, and went to a grammar school. She trained as a nurse and qualified as a state registered nurse in 1975. She has one daughter, Yvonne, aged eleven. She is not married. At present she lives and works as a nurse in Plymouth.

Pauline Heap is thirty-two. She was born in Newport, Monmouthshire, but grew up in Bristol. She went to a Roman Catholic high school and left when she was seventeen. She joined the WRNS in 1961 and married in 1963. She left the WRNS in 1964 when she became pregnant. Her first daughter died aged one week, and she later had a son, Colin, who is twelve, and a daughter, Joanne, who is seven. Pauline's husband sued her for divorce when she started her relationship with Pauline Willert and was granted a decree nisi in October 1975. He contested Pauline's custody of the children although he did not want custody himself. After over a year of welfare and medical reports, Pauline is waiting for the decree absolute and custody. At present she lives with Pauline Willert in Plymouth with their three children and works as a clerk in Plymouth dockyard. Both Paulines are active in their local CHE group.

* Where did you meet?

W: I was a student nurse and I was allocated to an orthopaedic ward and Pauline was a ward clerk. I hated the sight of her at first – I didn't hate the sight of her really, but I thought, God . . .

stuck-up bitch! For about six weeks I had that opinion, didn't I? And then we went out . . .

H: You invited me out.

W: No, you invited me out for a drink with the sister, didn't you?

H: Yes, a very close friend of mine, who was sister on the ward.

W: And I tried everything to get out of it, and Pauline said, 'There's no excuse, we'll go to the nearest boozer to where you live' – so I went home to my mother and father and said, 'I've got to go out – I've been sort of cornered – I've got to go out with the sister and that bloody ward clerk,' and I said, 'I don't want to go.' We had a smashing evening, didn't we?

H: Yes.

* Were you both married when you met each other?

W: No, I've never been married. I was living with my mother and father.

H: I was married, living in married quarters with my ex-husband, he's in the Navy. And like Pauline, when I first saw her I thought, Oh God, I don't like her. You were always looking daggers at me when I used to come in in the morning . . .

* How long had you known each other before you realized you were attracted to Pauline?

H: About five months. I remember we got awfully drunk one night and she'd stopped the night before, and this particular night I had to undress her and put her to bed. [*Laughter.*] I didn't do anything, but I was very tempted to – I thought, Pauline, stop it, pull yourself together – you're not queer – this is ridiculous, and I must admit I put her to bed and I had to go downstairs and have a drink and sit down and have a cigarette and I thought, Oh . . . no . . . you just want to try something new, that's all, and I talked myself out of it. We went on like this for ages . . . I was always frightened – I suddenly realized the way I was feeling about her – I thought, No, well she'll never speak to me again, I'll lose her friendship as well, which was very dear to me. In the meantime, I moved down to Plymouth.

W: I fancied her like hell, but I was too scared to say anything.

* Had either of you had relationships with women before?

W: I had one – it was really what triggered Pauline off – she was

6

so damn mad when she found out about it – I went out . . . I was very good pals with this woman actually – our daughters went to the same school, and she lived just up the road from me. We went out to celebrate her birthday, I got absolutely blotto and when we got back she started making advances to me – I was a bit amazed but I thought, OK, I'll try it – there was no love in our relationship – it lasted a month – it was purely sexual . . . and exciting really, I suppose . . .

H: This was during the time we were fancying each other. I was living in Plymouth and this happened in Gillingham in Kent. It was the Sunday lunchtime you rang up and told me . . . I was so mad . . .

* You were really jealous, were you?

H: Yes – I was so angry . . . I thought, God – maybe I've lost her after all, by not doing anything – by doing something I was frightened of losing her – by not doing anything it looked then as if I'd lost her anyway. I wrote her a rather – what did I put in my letter? I thought Ann was the wrong girl anyway for her . . .

W: Yes. You said you weren't ashamed – I'd said I wasn't ashamed of what I'd done, it was something new, it was an experience, and Pauline said she wasn't angry, but she felt I'd chosen the wrong person and I thought, Oh! So I said, Ohhh . . . Why didn't you say that a few months ago? [*Laughter*.]

H: We'd come close to it – and all our friends thought we were . . .

W: We were such good friends and we used to go out and lark around, and if we went out and there were fellows bothering us who we really didn't fancy, we used to pretend we were, just to get rid of them.

* Had either of you before this ever thought you were a lesbian, or ever thought about it?

W: Yes – I did, certainly – I had a Swedish pen pal – this was ten years ago. I thought, Golly, she's nice, I rather fancy her, then I thought, Don't be so bloody silly, you can't fancy another woman, it's ridiculous.

H: No. I don't think I ever thought I was – I was always known for looking at page three of the *Sun* – this type of thing. I used to admire the female body, but I never really stopped to think about whether I was a lesbian. I was so busy with my heterosexual life that I never really considered it at all – even though I'd done three years in the Wrens – even then. Maybe I was a little bit naïve – I was a virgin until I was nineteen and maybe this is part of it. I mean I did two years in the Wrens before I lost my virginity. When I first joined up I had a very nice PO Wren who everybody said fancied me and I wouldn't have it . . . she was smashing and she never made advances towards me, and yet I could get around her any way I wanted – if I wanted time off, leave or anything.

* Were you aware of other women having affairs in the Wrens?
H: Oh yes – as I advanced further. On one occasion I had to do the rounds with the Second Officer, and I'm afraid I had to run in two girls for lesbian activities, which is illegal – there was nothing else I could do – I felt very sorry to have to do it, but I had no choice, I had a superior officer with me, and I had to go and stand up in front of the Captain and say what I'd seen. We caught these two girls in bed, and it was very sad, and I felt very distressed over doing it at the time . . . I tried not to say anything detrimental against them at the hearing. One girl was discharged and the other girl was kept in . . . The active partner, as they call it, was discharged.

* How do they decide who is the active partner?
H: I don't know – maybe because she was more butch.

* How did you two finally get together?
H: We booked up to take the children on holiday to Butlin's for a week . . . Romantic!
W: . . . and it was West Camp W8.
H: A year ago last June – June 8th, our wedding anniversary . . .

* W8 is the name of the room?
W: Yes, the chalet.
H: We sort of avoided each other for most of the week . . .
W: Well – I didn't know what to expect when I met you.
H: I didn't mention anything . . .
W: She never mentioned it – coming down on the train I thought, Christ, I'm going to get my ears pounded over this, but she never mentioned it. The only remark she made was when we got to the

camp and went in the chalet – the kids were sleeping in one bedroom and there was a double bed in the other one, and she looked at me and said, 'I don't think much of these sleeping arrangements.' [*Laughter*.] I thought, Oh Christ.

H: Go on . . .

W: We had a very nice week, really. On the Wednesday night I couldn't bear it much longer. I thought, My God – I'm going to do something desperate in a minute. We'd been out and had a few drinks – she was obviously teasing me and she said, 'What's the matter – what's troubling you?' and I said, 'I'll tell you presently,' and I thought, How the hell am I going to tell her? I must say something, and she said, 'I'm just going to the loo,' and I thought, When she comes back I'll tell her – and then she fell asleep. [*Laughter*.] It was a long time before I went to sleep that night. The following day we went on the beach and she teased me like mad – got the suntan oil out and said, 'Would you like me to rub this on your back?' and I felt like: I'd love you to; but I behaved like: Get off! Leave me alone; and then you invited me to rub some on your back, didn't you, and continued to torment hell out of me for the rest of the day. It finally happened on the Thursday, Thursday, the 13th of June . . .

H: I must admit I was teasing her, but I felt the first move had to come from her.

* Why?

H: She'd already had a relationship – and to be quite honest I just didn't know how to start – I was so scared – I tend to shut myself up and hide my feelings inside and sort of be outrageous on the outside – which I was, and on Wednesday I thought, Ah . . . she's going to tell me how she feels, and then I fell asleep. I think it's an escape with me to fall asleep. On the Thursday – beach – I really was pushing her to try and persuade her to say something, if only I don't fancy you – end of story. Well – we'd been out for a few drinks – I got quite . . . I was screaming – we went to bed and I said, 'Is it going to be another night of "I'll tell you presently"?' – you carry on, you remember it better than I do . . .

W: I said, 'Well, you're troubling me a great deal,' or something like that . . . We mentioned my other affair, didn't we? I said, 'I'm

9

too scared to touch you,' I said, 'I'm sorry . . . Yes . . . I fancy you but I'm just terrified' . . . I was scared that if I did anything wrong it would end – it had been a lovely friendship for eighteen months and just for the sake of one false move – you know . . . we eventually got down to it, didn't we?

H: I can never explain that night – it was soul-shattering. I never realized I could feel that way – never before – it was so . . .

W: We had another week, didn't we? We went back to Plymouth and we had another week together before we had to go home again. And it was hell having to leave, I mean it always was anyway, but especially then, and we went to Bristol, didn't we, to see your mother?

H: Yes.

W: It was three or four weeks later . . .

H: And my in-laws guessed – apparently they'd guessed then at Bristol – how we felt towards each other – we couldn't hide it, no matter where we went we couldn't hide our feelings – we kept trying to push it off – no, we can't feel like this, it's just something new – but it wasn't, we both knew that.

W: We thought, How do we explain – or tell people? Pauline's married with two kids and I've got a daughter, and I'd been pregnant twice besides having a daughter. But then we just – really, we just couldn't go through with it.

H: Things got worse and worse.

W: And when we were apart it was terrible – so we decided, Yes, we'd tell people.

H: And we'd start by telling Philip, my ex-husband.

W: At first he thought it was a great idea – he understood – he said he understood, so we were quite happy, and then we realized the reason he understood was that he thought he could not only have Pauline, he could have me too. When he realized that I loved Pauline it shattered him – he couldn't believe it. He said, 'You love her and you don't love me,' and I said, 'I never loved you – not the way I love her,' and he just couldn't accept it. And he made our lives a torment – we had months of when we were apart and doubts. I thought maybe it was too much for her to take on to come down here – I was worried about the children – we started buying another house and that fell through – we started buying this one, but I knew then that there was only one –

our 'someday' we called it, it would have to come – there was no other way out.

W: We wrote letters, we were on the phone . . .

H: We tried to split up – we tried – I went to see a psychiatrist . . . my doctor had advised me to go.

* Did you receive any help from psychiatrists or doctors?

H: No, I don't think so. He told me that I'd accepted myself and it was getting others to accept me – I no longer needed him. In fact I didn't ever need him at all because I'd accepted that I was a lesbian in my mind, it was a case of trying to get other people to accept me. Some days it was terrible – I could never see any end, no ending at all. I was adamant, the way I felt. He said did I feel that I wanted to sleep with my husband, and I said, no, I didn't, that in fact we'd started sleeping in separate beds.

W: We decided to tell my parents.

* What was their reaction?

W: My father at first understood, or he said he did, but when my mother found out she called us disgusting creatures, and said we needed to see a doctor and that we needed pills, so I suggested that she buy us some Bob Martin's anti-mate pills if she thought that would do us any good. She said that she'd be prepared to understand or even accept it if we'd both been single and never been with a man – never had children – she could accept it.

* God – did you ask her why?

W: No – she wouldn't talk, you see, she just flew up in a rage, didn't she, that one night. Refused to speak about it or anything – she told me to get out – she wanted me to get out, and I said, 'No, I've got my State Finals coming up, and I'm not getting out until after the results.'

* And what's her attitude now?

W: She's completely disowned me, my father has too.

* And your mother has as well, Pauline?

H: Yes. As far as my in-laws are concerned, I'm dead and buried, and a lot of my friends . . .

* Did you come out openly to all your friends?

H: I told my friends, yes. Once I'd come out in the smallest possible way, there was no other alternative for me than to be honest with everybody. I couldn't hide it – I don't hide it at work – I don't know whether they know or not, I don't go around saying, 'I'm gay, that's it, you've got to accept it,' but they know I live with Pauline and they know I've recently been divorced. I think most of them know and they just take it as something that's happening.

* Are you out of the closet at work, Pauline?

W: Oh yes, they know, yes . . .

* You haven't had any trouble?

No.

* That's great.

W: I came out of the closet beautifully; I've never hidden the fact that I live with Pauline, I always talk about ours as a family – Pauline and the children. Why should I hide it, I'm not ashamed? Last week I asked the staff nurse to type up the CHE constitution, and I rang her up and said, 'It's Pauline here, do you know anyone who can type?' and I said, 'Well we've got something we want typed,' and she said, 'What is it?' and I said, 'A constitution,' and she said, 'What for?' and I said, 'The Campaign for Homosexual Equality,' and she said, 'Oh I see,' so I said, 'Well, I'm glad you do.' 'I'll do it for you,' she said.

* Well, you both obviously have a very together family scene, don't you – you're very close . . .
W: We've had our ups and downs.
H: We've had our rows.
W: I never thought it possible that we'd ever row, but since we came to live down here, we've had our rows . . .

* What happened about your divorce, Pauline?
H: We went to a solicitor together to decide what we were going to do. And the solicitor took Philip's side completely – he was surprised that I wanted the children. The next thing I knew was a petition naming Pauline as my lover, and saying that he would no longer be required to live with me, and mentioning the fact that I had a homosexual relationship with another woman. So, we took the petition and went down to see a solicitor, and he went to court. We didn't appear in court – we were waiting around to go – and the decree absolute ordered that there be welfare reports, and also psychiatrists' reports on the children. He wasn't happy with the situation – apparently Philip had got up and said that Pauline was an evil influence on the children and that was about it. Then we had a letter from the Probation Service – the welfare officer wanted to come and see us – and he came to talk with me – he didn't want to speak with Pauline at first, and I spent two and a half hours of very thorough grilling in here one evening. From the start of my marriage – all what I'd been through – apparently he'd spoken to Philip that same afternoon – he wanted to hear my version. He was quite surprised to hear I'd had relationships outside my marriage – I don't know how much my husband had said to him, but I put him in the picture about beatings-up from my husband during our married life, right up to the point where he offered for Pauline to come and live with us providing he could have a threesome with us.

* And he hadn't said any of this?
H: No, he hadn't mentioned any of this.

* Were you in love with him when you got married?
H: No, I wasn't.

* Why did you get married?

H: Because he was the first man I'd ever been to bed with.

* You felt you should?

H: Yes. I'd been brought up to think that way, and I got married – I felt sorry for him. I got to the stage where I thought I had to go through with the marriage. I didn't want to let anyone down, and the one person I was letting down was myself by getting married. But, then, if I hadn't got married I would have done something different and then I'd never have met Pauline.

* How do you feel about sex with men now, since you met Pauline?

H: I don't want to know – not at all.

* What about you Pauline?

W: No. No more . . .

* Tell us about your relationships with men.

W: I had lots of relationships with fellows, and I'd never been completely satisfied. I always wondered why – I thought there must be something wrong with me. The first time I saw my daughter Yvonne's dad I thought, He's nice, I'd like to get to know him – I went out with him for about a year – he was married – I knew he was married, although he told me he wasn't. It didn't make any difference, I still wanted him – I wanted his kid and I had his kid.

* Why do you think that a lesbian sexual relationship is more satisfying to you?

H: Because you understand each other more. I've always found men – although some of them want to try and please you . . . the main thing they're concerned about is their sexual pleasure, not the other person's. I think that's the basic ingredient in our relationship, to want to please the other more than yourself.

W: It's much more the same wavelength.

H: You've experienced the same feelings yourself, and you know how the other one will react.

W: We've had a lot of problems really, on my part more than yours. Not before I came to live down here, but since – there have been times when I just couldn't bear Pauline to touch me. I can't explain why – it wasn't that I didn't want her – I don't know what it was – but we've got over that problem now . . .

* What was the result of the psychiatrist's report?
W: We're still waiting till he's finished his report on Pauline and the children.

* And what about your daughter?
W: No, they're not interested in Yvonne because she's not directly concerned in the divorce.

* Isn't that insane?
H: Yes, it makes you laugh. It has to do also with what Philip has said about the children being down here with Pauline and the fact that we're members of CHE. Philip can't look after the children.

* Are they going to take them away from you, do you think?
W: No – not now.

* So Philip's position has been that although he can't have the children, he doesn't want you to have them either?
H: Yes. He told me he'd rather see them in care.
W: He's got a career in the Navy. He's not going to throw all that up for the children.

* Tell us something about your life together here, now you're together and fairly secure with having the children and so on – what kind of things you do, your social life and so on. How much time do you have?
W: We both work full time, and it's hard going at the moment. We'll be a lot happier when this welfare report is through, and the probation chap said as far as he can see the children will stay with us, and we'll have a supervision order made by the court and we'll have welfare officers coming round every six months to keep an eye on us.

* What effect do you think that all this has had on the children?
H: They're happier than they used to be – everything backs that up – their school work – everything backs up the fact that they are happier living here with us than they were living with me and my husband.

* Do they understand about your relationship?
H: We're open in front of them.

W: But they don't understand it fully. They don't understand the actual ins and outs of it all, but we sleep together and the children know this – they trot in and out in the mornings.

* Do they ever ask you questions?
W: Not as yet, really – we had a sex talk with them, didn't we?
H: Yes, a couple of months back . . .
W: Where do babies come from and all this, and Colin was very upset, he thought he could have a baby, and when he found he couldn't, he said he wasn't going to get married if he couldn't have a baby himself. We were reading them books and showing

them pictures, so Yvonne said, 'Do you mean men put that in there? That must be very uncomfortable!' [*Laughter*.]
H: She said that means you must have had it in there once, and I must have had it in there twice. [*Laughter*.]

* Did you mention homosexual sex at all?
W: Yvonne said, 'A man can love a man and a woman can love a woman can't they?' So we said, 'Yes.' 'But they can't have babies, can they?' And we said, 'No,' and that was the only reference as

yet. I mean, obviously there are going to be questions and questions.

H: They're saying things like, 'You love my mummy and my mummy loves you,' and that kind of thing.

* Are you going to tell them when . . .?

W: Yes.

H: I think if you're open – we don't hide it from them.

* Do you think perhaps they don't know you're what's called a lesbian?

W: No, they don't understand.

H: They don't know that society thinks it's wrong – that's the only answer to that question. As far as they're concerned, it's right that we live together and that's it.

* You obviously have a very loving atmosphere between the two of you and also from the two of you towards the children and back again, and you seem to have a good relationship, Pauline, with Yvonne.

W: It's been difficult – I think she's coming round now – she's been awkward, she still is at times, isn't she?

H: She can be very awkward.

W: I think it's because I've never been married, and she's had almost my full attention for eight and a half years of her life . . .

* Well, that would happen even if you were living with a man.

W: Yes, it would. She's very jealous at times, but she's got to accept it.

H: I don't think she's jealous so much of you, she's jealous of the attention she might be missing from both of us by the attention we show to each other.

* Do you think that they miss the masculine influence?

H: I don't think so – no. But then again, if I'd just left my husband to live alone, then I would not necessarily start living with a man – a lot of women bring up children on their own, and there's nothing wrong with that.

W: This is something the welfare chappie was on about – women being the influence in the house, with reference to Colin, and I said if we were two single-parent families living in the same house it would be different.

* What did he say to that?

W: He didn't have very much answer, did he? I sort of threw it straight back at him – without the single-parent families we'd have been lost, wouldn't we? But he has been very good, he's been very understanding.

H: He was very anti at first.

* You're involved in CHE – how did that first start?

H: When I found out I was homosexual I wanted to find out all there was to know about it, so the first thing I did was to try and find out what organizations, what magazines, what books there

were to read on lesbianism, so we joined CHE last October, and started a local group in January. We became quite involved in the start of it down here. I like the gay boys – it would be nice if we got some more women, but it's very difficult, they won't come out like in the big cities. Although Plymouth is quite big we're very sort of backwater down here. But we still plod on.

* Do you feel the need for more female gay companionship?

H: It would be nice – yes – to discuss things, things we can't really discuss with the lads really – it would be nice to make comparisons between life-styles.

W: We know two who have been together for three years – they have children too.

* Are they the only gay women you have any contact with? What about in the clubs you go to?
W: They all seem to be much younger than us. The older lesbians tend to stay home more, perhaps because there aren't many clubs here, and maybe they're more frightened to come out in the open.

* You two are quite in the open about it. You're not afraid.
W: No. We're basically honest people. If people don't like what we are they can go and . . .
H: It's surprising what people *don't* notice. When we go shopping with the children, we always hold hands or link arms, and nobody notices.

* Do you think you'd be happier in a big city like London, where there's a bigger lesbian scene?
H: I don't think I'd like to be living in London permanently.
W: I like to go out, but I'm a homely type really.

Veronica Pickles

Veronica Pickles is twenty-seven. She was born in Isleworth. As a student midwife she was sacked from her course for being gay. She received a lot of publicity in the national press and was eventually reinstated. At present she lives and works in Milton Keynes.

* The first thing we really wanted to ask you was, since all the publicity and having been sacked and rehired and all of that . . . What sort of effect has the whole thing had on people around you . . . people you worked with, patients and so on?

As far as colleagues go, they're a bit cagey at first, but as soon as they get to know me, it's all right. They talk a lot . . . come out with all the usual things. The tutors are careful of what they say in specific areas and my actual group at college I get on very, very well with. There's not one there now (last term was different) who puts me down at all, which I think is pretty good.

* Have they been supportive to you?

Some of them. I had a big hassle last term as I wanted to stand for the Students' Union as the Health Visitors' representative, and, . . . two or three of them . . . one was a vicar's wife . . . banging her fists on the table . . . were getting very aggressive about it. I stood down in fact because really I felt the hassle in the long run wouldn't be worth it and I didn't have time. Otherwise it's fine. There's a good atmosphere there and I think they're much more aware now, they don't go blithely on as they did before.

* Were you actually having a relationship with another woman when it all happened?

Well, I'd just moved away from the woman I'd been living with for five years when it all happened. I've been through a series of rather unhappy relationships since then, some of which were my fault, some of which were the inability of the other person to accept what I was doing. It's not been fun at all.

* Why did you decide to come out so publicly?

I didn't really decide. I mean you don't think, Well right, today I'm going to come out publicly. I suppose it's coming into contact with 'out' gay people and realizing really what it was all about. Feeling my own self-oppression for the first time. Realizing my isolation. Decided to start a group, and it all escalated from there because I'm just stubborn and I wouldn't do what they told me, which was to keep quiet. You get beyond a certain point and you think, Why the hell, that's their problem, not mine. I didn't think they would do that much, but they obviously thought that I wouldn't do that much either.

* Who's they?
The Area Health Authority. I think they thought that – well – keep her off the course this year and that will be the end of our problems. But I didn't comply like that. Get your teeth in like a terrier . . . grrrr . . .

* Do you think it's important for lesbians to be out of the closet?
Yes. Not specifically lesbians. I think it's important for all homosexuals to be out of the closet.

* Why?
It's healthier individually, I mean, it reduces internal tension, literally from a health point of view. I also think that – oh dear, I can't put it into words . . . Unless people know they're lesbians – and let's face it, there are a lot of women who have no conception about their sexuality – unless the women who know their sexuality are prepared to come out and show it, then other sisters who are less fortunate with regard to education and perhaps have a degree of stubbornness . . . I think an 'out' lesbian has to be stubborn – otherwise they'll never stand a chance – they'll be like so many others. They'll marry at seventeen and have five children and realize at forty they've missed a lifetime of beauty with another woman.

* Do you think that homosexuals who are out of the closet are laying themselves on the line, though . . . rather on the firing-line?
Yes, of course they are, but you have to. The more that people do it . . . if every single homosexual in this country tomorrow was to step over that miserable line and say 'Here I am,' it would no longer be their problem. It isn't their problem when they do it anyway, but it's a problem of society accepting them – I think when somebody does step forward . . . the sense of release I had . . .

well, it wasn't my problem any more. If they didn't accept me then they could bloody well lump me! I don't, quite honestly, care. It's their problem. But it's also the problem of the homosexuals who haven't. I mean it's this self-oppressive thing as well.

* Well, it's fear, isn't it?
Yes, but what's the fear of? Is it fear of being exposed because they find themselves disgusting? And they'd hate other people to see how disgusting they are?

* It could be their fear of losing the stake in society that they've so carefully built up.
Yes, I think the basic fear is loss of position and identity in society.

* Loss of straight friends.
Loss of straight friends.

* There are homosexuals who've lost their jobs and there are ways of oppressing homosexuals within their jobs that aren't always apparent to the people who are being oppressed. There are lots of steps of advancement when they don't have to tell you why they've turned you down for the job.
Yes, that's right. It's the same in my profession. I'll never get higher than a health visitor as things stand at the moment.

* When you first came out, you were working as a midwife, weren't you? Mainly with women obviously. What kind of reaction did you have from the women you worked with, the patients?
My patients – very little when I was fighting the thing . . .

* None of them mentioned it to you?
One or two, in a roundabout sort of way. Two patients said they didn't want to see me – two out of quite a large number. I was working in Bletchley, which is a pretty large catchment area. After I won the course back and it was in all the papers, and it was a victory and all this sort of thing, I got cards, boxes of chocolates and flowers – all from patients saying, 'I'm glad you've won, sorry you won't be here to deliver my baby, thank you for the care you've given me,' etc., etc.

* How did you feel?
It was an added bonus really. I was fortunate, because I was in the position of being well known then, and there were enough people who knew me personally. I mean, if I'd been some cranky midwife

that worked in a maternity hospital ten miles away . . . this is why I think it's important when people come out, that they come out in a situation where they're already known, and then people . . . you can almost hear them saying, 'Well, she can't be that bad, because I've known her all this time.' This in itself is an oppressing thing to say, but this is how people see it. I think I was lucky in that situation, but I got beyond the point . . . I couldn't care . . . They had me . . . I was told . . . I was informed that they had me followed for a week . . .

* Who?

The Area Health Authority. To make sure I was doing my job properly, I suppose . . . To make sure I wasn't dropping off to screw a few women.

* Repulsive.

It was hell. I mean it really was bad, from that point of view. Among my immediate colleagues, the ones I actually worked with (we shared the work-load), the atmosphere wasn't bad. But in the maternity unit it was hell. If I was two minutes late at any time, or if I missed a delivery because I'd been out on calls, all this was brought up every time I was late. I missed three deliveries over a period of four months in the summer when it was really busy because I'd been busy working elsewhere. And once I'd gone home because the doctor said she'd be hours yet and I wanted some supper and she wasn't around . . . but these things happen to any midwife. Someone else was there to deliver it so there was no suffering involved, but they brought this up at the hearing too. Every single misdemeanour. It really showed how petty they were making it. They were picking on bits because they had nothing else to pick on. Anyway, that's all finished.

* I was going to ask how all this affected you personally – in your personal life and emotionally . . . the whole business. Were you frightened?
When I was called up to be actually kicked off the course . . . because I wasn't sacked you see. What had happened was that the Area Health Authority pays the money for you to do the course, and what they did was withdraw the financial backing. When they called me up to do that, I was called up to see my senior nursing officer and I ended up seeing the top knobs. I took Liz with me – the girl I lived with for five years – they wouldn't let her in. I was in there for an hour and they tried to get me to voluntarily withdraw and I wouldn't. I came out of there and I felt sick – I was so frightened I felt sick. The socialization process of a nurse is pretty tough; you are taught to bow to authority right, left and centre. What I did at that stage in time I wouldn't think twice about doing now, but it took a hell of a lot of courage because it was going against everything I'd been taught to do. In effect I told my superior to take a running jump. I told them I'd fight it, then I went home and collapsed for ten days – weeping and poking my head outside the door and not knowing what the hell to do. Then I really started fighting it. Private life, relationships it disrupted considerably, and I began to find that I was chased round by people who hadn't shown any liking for me before. You become well known and you find out who your friends are. It's very sad. It showed a side of human nature I didn't particularly want to see again. During that time the fight was going on there were lots of people running round supporting me, but as soon as I won they all

stopped. There was little old me: I was so depressed, so tired and so down, I had that bloody course to start, it was hell, awful. I think I must have gone through a period of four or five months of acute depression and a very unhappy affair in the interim.

* What's your perspective – your future now?
I want my freedom.

* What will you do when you've finished your course?
Well, I signed a contract with the government for two years. But if I'm lucky there's a chance that I might be able to do research during that time, but whatever I do, I'm not staying in nursing the rest of my life.

* Why?
Because I start to feel so aggressive, so angry.

* About what?
Attitudes. I cannot see myself as a tweed-wearing health visitor who goes round telling people how to look after their children.

* Well, do you think you're not going to run across attitudes like that in other areas? In a university or in some kind of medical research?
Oh yes, but the thing is that I'm in a situation where you're not encouraged to have independent thought. You go into the little sausage machine and come out at the end like everybody else – a nice health visitor. You are not encouraged to be individual. Once you start the job . . . I mean the bureaucracy of the Health Service is throttling, awful. The women you're meant to kow-tow to – the men too – the doctors.

* What do you think about the power of doctors in medicine, in women's medicine?
Pigs, butchers, sods, bastards, that's what I think. When I was doing my midwifery training, there was one registrar and there was this woman who was having an emergency caesarian. She was bleeding from the cervix and they tried to pack the vagina with swabs to put pressure on the cervix to stop it bleeding. Oh, he was a swine. He pulled back the bedclothes – this woman was still in a semi-lethargic state – and started pulling this stuff out as if he was pulling the innards of a dead sheep and he said to me, 'Can I have some more swabs, nurse?' so I gave them to him and watched him

stuff this woman. And when he'd finished I said to him, 'You're a pig, I pity any woman who becomes your wife.' And I wouldn't go with him to the patient again. I felt like getting the scissors and stabbing them in his face. I mean to treat any woman . . . well, I couldn't treat a dog like that. A bit of meat to be hacked about.

* What's it like for lesbians round here where you live?
Well the ones I know – oh hell, what's it like for lesbians anyway? All depends on the lesbians. A lot of them are the gay-scene type and most of them are in the closet, very much so.

* Well, it's much easier to be out of the closet and part of it some-where like London, isn't it?
Sure, because you're lost in the crowd, whether you're out of the closet or not. In an area like this you're often in a fairly small community and you stand out a lot, very much so. But there are some very aware women around this area and they're lovely people. I didn't realize how many lesbian couples there were tucked away in the back-woods and little manor houses.

* Have you met them through CHE?
Oh no. They won't go near CHE or the Women's Movement or anything that spells out 'exposure'.

* How did you dig them out?
I'm getting introduced to them now. I mean my circle has widened and they all seem very curious to meet this person called Veronica Pickles. They seem quite surprised when they realize I'm, you know, really quite nice to know and won't bite their heads off too much. But as I say, I'm still feeling terribly vulnerable in some ways as a result of what's happened. When people start on about how they are not being oppressed, I just find myself dissolving into tears because I feel so sorry for them because they are so logical and this is what's so horrifying. The arguments they put forward for their own self-oppression are so logical, and until they see it for themselves there is not a sod you can do. They just won't see it, and I usually end up crying or something.

* Why does it upset you so much?
Because it's such a waste – such a waste of people. Because people can never start to grow or to find their own limits. They don't ever get on the doorstep of it until they accept themselves and they

haven't accepted themselves. And they still allow the local men to come round and pinch their bottoms, and I find it all quite nauseating, painful and horrid – and frustrating because they won't listen – I mean they think I'm screwy.

* Have you ever felt ashamed?
I've never felt ashamed, although I did feel right at the beginning that it was wrong. I don't know if you can realize the difference between these two. I was frightened of being found out in case of what people might think. Because, I suppose, they'd think it was wrong. That was right at the beginning, because it was a very awkward situation. The first affair I had was with an alcoholic sister.

* How old were you then?
Nineteen. That was the first physical affair, and she was an alcoholic night sister and a raving lunatic. She was a right old lady. She is very sweet. She was on the wards that I was on as a student and she would ring me up and send me off to the path lab for blood and she'd be waiting there – and I'd come back two hours later with my cap on the back of my head and things. I was a nervous wreck. I mean, can you imagine it! Anyway, that was the start and

I was very frightened of people finding out because it would have ruined my career. When I look back, I realize that they all realized anyway. When I met Liz my attitude changed completely because I fell in love with Liz and I wanted to go and shout it and Liz was the one that wouldn't. And shame and everything dropped then and it took me four years to get Liz to come out and I couldn't come out without her. And she used to reinforce my own self-oppressive attitudes and I'd say, 'I'm fed up with all this, I'll tell the lot of them. Why the hell should we deny it?' And she'd say, 'I'd lose my job, I'd never get promotion,' and things like that.

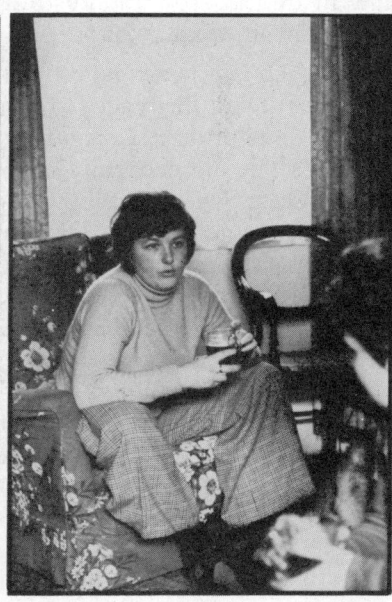

She's now a – she's grown, she's a fabulous woman now. She has really grown, she's not the same person.

* Well, people never usually are, are they? They usually change an awful lot when they come out.

But I think the first thing you have to do – only speaking from my own experience – I think some people almost have to be forced into a situation of coming out before they can see their oppression which will make them come out more. I think anyone with any depths to them at all can't do anything else but. It's like a hair shirt.

* It's so much easier to meet other lesbians if you're out of the closet too. You're so isolated when you're in the closet.

Quite honestly I think it's much easier to meet other people. You know, to meet one's own is important, but when you're in the closet you're socially restricted completely.

* You get into such complicated situations. Playing a charade.

That's right. Do you know – I don't mention the town in case they sue me – at a hospital I worked at they have, let me think now, one, two, three, four, five quite definite lesbians, and one quite probable, and all these just in administration, and there are eight administrators in all, women that is.

* Have you met many gay women nursing?

Oh yes. It takes them ages to admit it to each other. Lots of long intense pints of beer. [*Laughter.*] I don't have that problem now, it's nice. The big maternity hospital I worked at just prior to all this business, when I was working as a sister on district . . . they, of course, came in for a lot of questions about me because I'd worked there. And the gay women there spent the whole time saying, 'It's not the Veronica Pickles we know.'

* How many Veronica Pickles are there?

I don't know, but, of course, there could quite easily be another one who works as a midwife in Milton Keynes. You mustn't jump to conclusions, it might not be that poor girl. I mean she was such a nice girl, I'm sure it couldn't be her.

Judy Barrington

Judy Barrington is twenty-eight. She was born in Brighton, and went to school at St Mary's Hall, Brighton. She started studying psychology at London University, but dropped out. She has worked as a secretary at the BBC, an interpreter in Spain, a public relations executive in an advertising agency, a marketing director in an engineering company and in furniture removals. She was married in 1969 and separated in 1970.

* When did you come out of the closet?
When I joined the Women's Movement. About three and a half years ago. In the first women's group I was in, we eventually got around to talking about lesbians, and I had to admit to having had various affairs with women, and it was really the first time I had admitted it to myself.

* Had you actually had any sexual experiences?
I'd had affairs with four women before that, but each time I hadn't really thought about it in terms of being a lesbian. I just thought it was a kind of freak experience. That it was just a one-off thing. And in the middle of all that I got married, so I wasn't really admitting it to myself.

* So you had affairs with women before you were married?
Yes.

* And with men at the same time?
Yes.

* And what happened after that when your marriage fell apart?
Well – quite soon after I left my husband I began to get involved in the Women's Movement. I didn't know anything about it, but I came across the address of the workshop office and I went and found out a bit about what was going on, and they found me the address of a local women's group which I joined, and began to get a political consciousness about being a woman.

* Why were you interested when you heard about this group? What attracted you?
I have absolutely no idea. I think that in a very repressed way I really resented being a woman for years. I resented the way I was playing all these games about thinking I should get married. Because I'd been relatively free and independent for about five or six years – travelled a lot and been on my own. But I always thought that sometime I was going to have to settle down and do the right things, and I think I resented it a lot; and so, as soon as I began to hear any of the ideas about women's oppression, it made a lot of sense to me and I identified with it immediately.

* How did it change your life-style, becoming involved in women's politics?
It didn't immediately, but after about a year – I'd had a job, I was director of a company, and it began to feel impossible to go on because I was in a position of exploiting a lot of women –

* What was the company?
It was an engineering company. I began to see just how the women in the factory were really exploited, and the whole system, and how I'd just never seen any of it before. I didn't feel able to be part of it . . . for a while I had to get right out of it in order to be able to see clearly all the ways in which my mind had been fucked over up until then. So I gave up my job about nine months, I guess, after I first became involved in the movement. And it also changed my life in so far as I went to live in a women's house with other women, and at that time I was very idealistic, and I thought that it was really good to try and live communally with other women and set up women's houses and places where women could live together and not have to relate to men if they didn't want to.

* You say at that time you were very idealistic?
Well, I mean it was a lot harder than it seemed. When I first became involved in the movement it just seemed like it was a matter of acting on the ideas, but when I started to do it, I realized it was a lot harder than that. I mean I couldn't change all the ways I had been – had become in twenty-odd years.

* So did you go back to your job?
No I didn't – I did a lot of different kinds of work on and off in that time. Some women and I got together and set up an agency – an

employment agency for women which was there simply to try and get work for women which had been labelled men's work, the kinds of work that men always have the prerogative in. We had a lot of women carpenters, electricians – things like that. And I did some of that kind of work – I learned to do wiring and I also did removals and a lot of casual work in that time, just to earn enough money to live.

* What are you doing now?
I still live in a women's house and I'm writing and drawing social security – contemplating my future. I write poetry and also sometimes write political things, but not so much as I would like to.

* What sort of poetry?
About my life really – and, you know, what it's like to be a woman. I belong to a women's writers' group which I started with another woman about six months ago – because we both felt that we needed to get together with other women because I think a lot of women write and are sort of closet writers, and always have the idea that what they write is totally irrelevant because male publishers have these kind of standards – that what women write and women's lives and the things they write about are all trivial and unimportant and I think it's very important for women to be able to take themselves seriously as writers and to try and fight that, and to know that even if no one will publish them it's not necessarily because the publishers' standards are in some way the right standards. A little pamphlet of my poems has been done, and I think that some of the women I know who are learning to print eventually hope to get the equipment together to do much more of that.

* Have you ever belonged to any of those left-wing groups, like IMG, IS or the Workers' Revolutionary Party?
No. I came straight from being a completely straight reactionary dyed-in-the-wool Tory, to being relatively quickly a feminist; I didn't go through that left-wing political time at all.

* What do you think about the Women's Movement in relation to those kind of organizations? Do they have any relevance to women – to feminists?
No, they don't. I don't have a lot to do with them – I don't know a lot about the internal functioning of them – but it seems from the

35

little I have seen that the attitudes within the Left are very patriarchal and male and that the women are certainly servicing the men. I mean they may be servicing the male revolution, but they're in the same relationship to the men and I would imagine that it's of very little importance to women in terms of women improving their situation as a class. If you look upon women as a class, I don't think in fact that the Left is doing them any good.

* Can women achieve any real liberation under capitalism, though? That's the argument, isn't it? No, I don't think so, but I certainly don't think women are going to do anything to improve their situation by fighting capitalism for men or for a male organization.

* About the Women's Movement then? What's it like now?
I don't have a very objective perspective on the situation because I spent the whole of last year working in the workshop office, which is the central information office of the Women's Movement, and at that time I felt very much in the middle of things, and it felt as if there was an awful lot going on. I think that it probably always seems as if there's little going on to women who have never come into contact with anyone who's active because of the attitude that the media has to the Women's Movement, and because we've never adopted an attitude of trying to evangelize or actually systematically trying to get the media on our side or use the media for our purposes. So whatever we've done has been really very ignored in terms of how it's been seen by the world at large.

* Things like big women's marches are really quite noticeably ignored by the press, aren't they? Why do you think that is? Do you think it's a deliberate attitude or is it an accident?
I don't think any of it is an accident. I think that the media – the newspapers – are there to uphold various interests. Some of them uphold left interests and some of them uphold the establishment, but they're all there basically to uphold the interests of men, and it's not in their interests to say anything about what we're doing – and if they do they always trivialize it or make a joke of it. Because that's the only way it's really of interest to their readers.

* What's your opinion of the relationship between lesbian women and heterosexual women within the Women's Movement?
There was a national conference at which everybody discussed the subject of lesbianism and the relationship between lesbians

and non-lesbians and the Women's Movement adopted a demand for the movement which said that it would support lesbians and would fight the oppression of lesbians. And I think that because that happened, superficially the differences were patched over, but it hasn't really changed the situation in which there are many straight women who feel very threatened by the high proportion of lesbians in the movement. It's a very real problem because I can really sympathize with the situation of a woman who is first getting involved in the movement and is liable to be accused of being a, lesbian before she's ever even thought about it. Even though I had in fact had lesbian experiences, if that had happened to me when I first joined the movement, then I might not have got involved as quickly as I did. It's a real problem, but I don't really know how to solve it.

* Is it any easier for lesbians to see women's oppression clearly than for heterosexual women who are trapped in their various situations?
I don't really know what to say about that, and I don't feel that evangelical about being a dyke. I don't want to participate in trying to influence that aspect of another woman's life. Maybe that's because I have experienced being around some women when they've made those kind of decisions about changing their life-style and finally coming out as lesbians and when it's involved children and husbands. It's something that a woman has to be really sure about and decide on her own without using someone who is already a lesbian in order to make that decision.

* It's a lot easier for them to come out in the Women's Movement than to be a working-class dyke . . .
Yes, I think that's true, but I don't really consider that coming out. If I went to a Women's Movement national conference, stood up at a microphone and said, 'I'm a lesbian,' I don't think that's coming out at all. It's coming out when I go back to my straight conservative family and say, 'I'm a lesbian,' and they rush off and say, 'Well, we're going to call the bin and have you committed.' That's coming out.

* Did they? [*Laughter*.]
No – they haven't – but the feeling, or the fear that they might is what you have to go through if you're really going to come out,

37

and coming out is coming out in the world as it is, and not in some little ghetto or little section that accepts you anyway. There are a lot of people around who say they've come out, but what they mean is that they walk around with a lot of Women's Movement friends wearing a dyke badge which they take off if they go out of London. That's not really changing anything.

* Were you freaked out when you realized that you were a lesbian?
I wasn't really freaked out about it, I was mostly angry that I had walked around for so many years feeling that I had to hide it from myself and everybody else, and not admit that that was what was

going on, because life would have been a lot easier if I had come to terms with it a lot sooner. I feel very strongly that if I want to change anything it's that I want to change things enough so that a lot of other women don't have to do that.

* Can you remember being attracted to women when you were very young?
In retrospect, yes. In retrospect, I tend to interpret my friendships at school and when I was very young as having a dimension that I

don't think everybody else's feelings had. They used to be very important to me, and I used to get very mixed up about my feelings for women; and probably there was a sexual element to quite a lot of my important friendships with them, but I wasn't aware of that at the time.

* Are you living with a woman now?
No. I have a long-term committed kind of relationship with a woman, but we don't live in the same house, although we spend most of our time together.

* How long have you been together?
Just about three years now. With a gap of almost a year in the middle.

* Why don't you live together?
We have only recently seriously thought of living together. For a number of reasons – one of which was that we had a lot of conflicting views about being a couple or getting into a very tight relationship that meant we were in some ways acting very kind of married. We weren't very sure about the whole thing.

* We've been through that whole drama.
Being in the Women's Movement makes that very difficult because there's an awful lot of ideology against having very close couple relationships. There are a lot of women about who try to make you feel guilty about that. That's something that I've found quite difficult, especially as I've lived in houses with other women, and if I'm involved in a couple relationship with somebody who's not living in the house, it tends to make it quite difficult to be committed to the women I live with in the right way because I spend a lot of time outside. So that's one reason we haven't lived together. Another is that our circumstances were very different. I'm getting to the point where I want to have somewhere more settled to live. I want to have more routine and a fairly secure existence. Her situation is that when I met her she had been married for a long time and she had two children, and so she really wanted to experience being on her own and finding her own strength and having time to herself to do things that she'd never been able to do before.

* Are you both free to have relationships with other people?
Well . . . the theory and the practice have always been quite different.

39

At the beginning we both subscribed to the theory that we were not going to be possessive, that we would allow each other the kinds of freedom that we thought should exist. But we found in practice that it was really very difficult – that we both got very hurt by it.

* If you live with someone for a long time, you are going to want to be with someone else or to fancy them or feel attracted to them sexually and emotionally . . . and yet what's the difference between thinking it and doing it?

Well, I think there is a difference – if I have a fantasy about somebody, it's very different than if I actually go off and sleep with them.

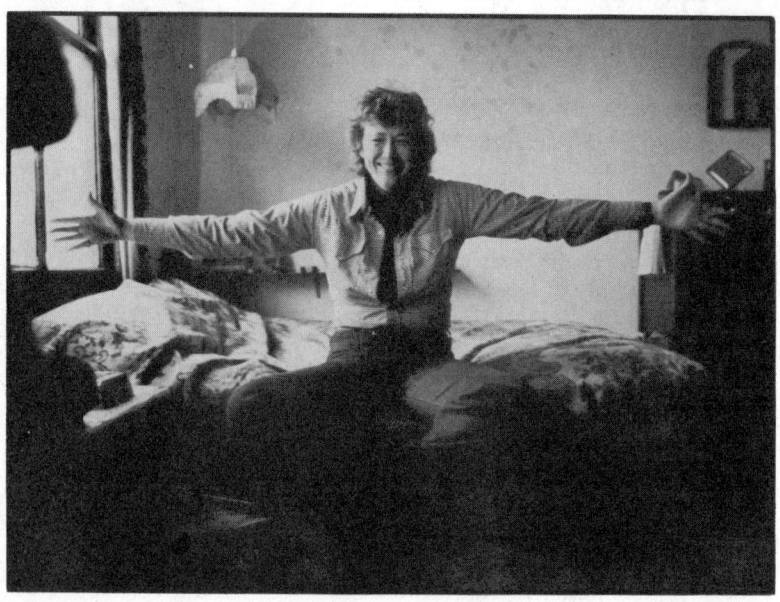

I really subscribe to what you're saying. I really think it's unrealistic to suppose that your emotions are going to stay wholly focused on one person. If you want to be a whole person, that's not how I would function. One of the problems specifically about being gay is that you already start with a lot of disadvantages because there is a lot of insecurity in relationships. Basically, every time I'm together with a woman I'm involved with, it's a choice every time. It's not because we're in any way connected in the view of society . . . we don't have anything to keep us together except a choice every time.

Janet Clark

*Janet Clark is thirty-two. She was born in
Stepney and went to a secondary modern in
Stepney Green. She left school at fifteen and went
to work as a washer-up in Joe Lyons, Leicester
Square. Later she did factory work in the East
End. At fourteen Janet was sent to a remand
home for five weeks for shoplifting, and was then
put on probation for two years. In 1973 she was
sent to Holloway for four months for obtaining
goods by deception, and then to an open prison,
where she stayed for nine days and then absconded.
She was sent to Styal Prison for four months. In
1975 she was given a two years' suspended
sentence for the same offence. Janet has a son,
David, aged nine, and a daughter, Debbie, aged
seven. She lives with them in a council flat in
Kilburn on £14.90 social security. She is not
married.*

* Have they ever asked you anything about you being a dyke?
What, the kiddies, you mean?

* Yeah, your kids.
No, not yet, but they've got their ideas, 'cos Debbie often says to
me, 'You never wear women's clothes, you always like to wear
jeans, shirts, socks and what-have-you,' and I says, 'Oh, that's the
way I like to be, Debbie.' I says, 'I like to feel as though I'm a fella,
which I know I'm not really, but I like to think I am one.' She just
laughed, anyrate, when I said that.

* Have you had a woman staying with you or sleeping with you,
have they ever come in?
I've had a few women friends staying, yeah.

* But they haven't realized that there was anything going on?
Well, funnily enough, you know, David says to me one day, 'You
never have men friends sleeping with you, do you?' so I happen to

say to David, 'It's just that I prefer women to sleep with me rather than have men sleeping with me.'

* Did he say, 'Why?'
No, funnily enough he didn't ask. I was expecting the question to come out, like.

* He took it as a natural thing, just something that someone preferred, I suppose.
It's true. I was expecting it, but he didn't, he just laughed, anyrate.

* So your attitude is that when they ask you, you are going to tell them?
Oh definitely, it's my place to tell them I think, anyrate.

* You're not married, Janet, are you?
No.

* You've never had any trouble with people from Social Security or child care or anything like that?
No, I haven't, no. I did talk to the child guidance woman myself one day because David was giving a lot of trouble at school like, so they thought he might need help like, seeing a child guidance counsellor or what have you. But they found he was all right, they just found it was behaviour anyway. He just likes to be noticed a lot, you know; so anyway, I just had to take confidence in her and tell her straight out what I was and she said to me, 'It's nothing to be afraid about these days,' 'cos she was wanting to tell me there was teachers, nurses and what have you that are gay. So she says, 'There's nothing to be worried about at all,' so I says, 'I thought I'd tell you this in case others might find out and then start saying I'm not fit to be a mother because I'm a lesbian.' So she says, 'I don't see why you're not fit to be a mother, there's nothing wrong with being a lesbian. It's not like years ago you were classed sick in the head or something like that, it's quite acceptable now.'

* We were talking about your kids and families. I thought we might ask you about your parents and your own family life, when you were a kid, like. Do you have any contact with your parents?
No, I don't.

* Do they know you are gay?
Well, my mother had an idea say, when I was, say, from fourteen onwards, because I'd realized from when I was quite a young

kiddie actually, but say thirteen when I knew truthfully what I was.
'Cos when I was smaller, I always wanted to do things that boys
wanted to do, like football, wearing shirts and jeans, never wanting
to wear dresses. My sister was a different kettle of fish altogether,
proper little prim she was. Not like me, a real tomboy. People used
to say to my Mum, 'That should have been a boy that one.' 'Cos
there was five boys before me, say five brothers, so I was the first
girl to come along, but that's got nothing to do with it, anyrate.

* Why don't you see your Mum now?

Well, no, I . . . I just had a big bust-up with my mother when I was
about sixteen and left home and not bothered since. I got so pissed
off I just left. I would have done something really bad, you know.
Could have turned on my mother, I think, in the end, because of
her attitude. I just don't know if it was this man that was domineer-
ing her, he was getting the better of her, why she went that way,
you know.

* Had you had any relationships with women?

Well, I did meet up with this girl now. Met up with her in a coffee
bar.

* How old were you then?

Going on for seventeen say, I was. Just a place I used to go to every
day, right, to get my meals and that. 'Cos I never used to bother
cooking or nothing, so 'cos I see this girl every day I just thought,
Ooh, I might as well make friends, I thought, than be on my own.
So it was just ordinary, casual friendship at first, and then I got to
feel as though I fancied her, you know. So I thought, Well now, I
thought to myself one day. How can I go about telling her that I
fancied her? I don't want her to start getting shocked or pulling
words that I am going to rape her or something. So I waited till I'd
had a few drinks one night and I just says to her like, 'Oh,' I says
like, 'it's just like this,' I says, 'I'm beginning to like you more and
more, you know, which might sound stupid,' I says. But I says to
her, 'I want to tell you something about myself as a friend, so if
you want to go against me, it's up to you.' But I just says to her, 'I
happen to be a lesbian and I really like you,' you know, and I
found to my surprise she wasn't shocked at all, which turned out to
be a coincidence – she was one herself, and she had the same feeling.
[*Laughter*.] What a coincidence, you know, because I'd had other

affairs off and on like, but this one I really got to like, and this happened to be Joyce now. Moved in for two years.

* Do you think you are born that way, or it's something that happens in your life and makes you a dyke?
I think I was born that way because it was something I realized when I was quite young. I liked girls, and if I was going to change now, I'm sure I would have changed after having the kids. Yeah, I'm sure about that, but I know I'm a lesbian.

* Did you ever have any heavy scenes with Joyce about jealousy and stuff like that?

Oh yeah, there used to be a lot of that in it, which was a very bad thing. I think it spoilt the relationship actually.

* And what about now, do you think you'd be jealous now in a relationship?
Well, I guess I'd get that jealous thing about me, but who wouldn't, but not as bad as before, not possessiveness, which is a very, very bad thing.

* Why do you think that?

Well, if one gets very, very possessive, the other one is going to think, She doesn't trust me. Now why the hell is it that she doesn't trust me? What am I doing that she doesn't trust me? – Getting suspicious all the time, you know.

* Yeah. Well, what you said earlier about your conversation with Debbie . . . I mean, it struck me as a funny thing to say to her in a way, because if she had said it to me for instance, I would have said 'because they are comfortable, and I like them and they are tough clothes and they last a long time,' but you said because

they make you feel like a man, although you know you're a woman. Yeah, that's true that, it's confusing, isn't it?

* Is that what being a lesbian is about to you? I mean . . . or is that just something else?

Well, I just . . . I think I tend to find I've got more male tendencies in me, you know.

* In what way, what kind of male tendencies?

Well, in lots of ways, you know. I feel as though I'd like to do the

47

things men want to do. But when it comes to clothing, I guess I'm in the same category as you, really. I feel more comfortable in them. I just wouldn't feel right in a dress, I wouldn't.

* Why is that, Janet?

Well, it's not a craze or how you call it. I feel as though . . . I'd feel like a right freak-out or something wearing a dress. I just prefer to wear trousers and shirts, because I find them more comfortable. I feel as though I'm me, you know, myself like and nothing special, although I know I'm different, you know, just me, I like wearing trousers, socks, shirts, underpants.

* Well, you know about the butch and femme and all that stuff that we talk about, you know, that dykes . . .

I saw something not long ago in a book on that.

* What do you think about it? Would you describe yourself as a butch?

Well I think now I class myself as a dyke, now that I come to think of it. I'm beginning to believe that there's no such . . . that there shouldn't be a thing of butch and femme like and all the rest of it. Of course, a few years ago I would have classed . . . I always liked to go as the butch. Now I just feel ordinary. I was the butch with Joyce which could have been wrong.

* Are you out of the closet – does everyone know about you?

Yeah, I would say so now. In the last two years I've really come out of the closet.

* Why did you come out of the closet? What made you want to do it?

Well, I suppose . . . I suppose it's just the fact that gay is being more accepted, you know, and a lot of gays are doing it, so I suppose it makes you more confident. I mean I came out the closet in a very quick way, not that I want to prove myself any better or any different, it's just that I just want to prove myself. If a lot more dykes done it, it would be accepted more.

* Right. Easier for the others.

Mmmm, yeah.

* What effect has it had on your life, like your friends, neighbours, all that kind of thing?

Well, a lot of people have quite accepted me and others have just gone against like. Although they've not said it like, openly you know, you can tell. I kind of find a lot of people have accepted it, which really surprised me.

* How do you feel about it now? Was it the right thing to do?
Well, I'm happy – I'm happy with it, the fact that I brought myself out and told people straight out that I'm a lesbian.

* We were going to ask you about in the nick too. Do you mind talking about it?
No, I don't mind.

* When did you first go in there?
Oh, I was about . . . let's see now. Say about ten years ago was the first time I was up and did six months, so that would make me twenty.

* Yeah, and you were a dyke then, of course?
Oh, yeah.

* And did you have any homosexual experiences in prison?
No, they were very strict on it then funnily enough, in the nick. If they thought for a minute two girls were having a lesbian affair, they would separate them, and if the rooms got too crowded up, they'd always put three into a cell. They tried to stop lesbianism, but now it's okay, now, in Holloway. Now you get a lot of these so-called girls which we class as nick vamps like, that can't get a man outside.

* Nick vamps?
Nick vamps is an expression like. When they've been in there long enough they get frustrated, they're writing letters to the butches and one thing and another. 'Cause one girl asked me to pass this letter to a butch one when she fancied her, and this butch was only laughing her head off at her, you know, and she passed the letter on to me afterwards and she said to me, 'Don't say nothing, 'cause I know what they're like, they're only frustrated, anyrate.' You know, we used to laugh over it, the butches did.

* These are dykes who get put in there, they're not straight at all?
No, no, they're definitely butch, you know. They're gay outside as well.

* And they're popular?
Oh, they are very popular . . .

* Do they manage to get off with each other in prison?
Oh, yeah, it's done now, like I said to you, it's accepted now.

* In Holloway?
Paired up together now.

* Two in a cell?
Yeah, like every Saturday you can change your cells if you want to, like. You just go to the PO on the wing and say, 'Warden, can I move in with so and so?' and all the screws know what's going on, they take no notice, they don't bother now, you know.

* So if you fancied someone, or you've fallen for someone and you want to like live with them, you can go and ask to be in the same cell as them?
Yeah, that's it, you just say I want to move out. It's not like it was ten years ago, you know.

* I wonder why it's changed. How many times have you been inside?
Twice.

* How long was the last time?
Last May I came out after twelve months, and that's when I found out it was a lesbian paradise.

* Well, did you have any affairs with women then while you were there?
I did have an affair with a girl then. When I first met her we just . . . well, she was a new girl, not long come to the wing.

* Was she a dyke?
Well – well, you're never going to believe this – now I'll tell you this as I go a bit further along. I take her to be a bisexual – although she says she was a lesbian. She'd had two kids herself, but she was divorced from her husband and one thing and another, right. Anyrate, it just started off just as an ordinary friendship, just talking, how's your past life and all the rest of it, and she says, in conversation, come down to her cell like. You know, come down to her cell and just talked – then she just happened to say to me, I mean just out of the blue she happened to say to me, 'You're gay,' and 'cause she had all writing and stuff on the wall and I thought dare I ask her, and I thought I don't want her to think I'm pushing myself onto her or something. So, I says to her, 'Hey, did you do

all them writings up there?' like, you know, just thought I'd make a sudden sweep of the cell like in the association, and she says, 'Yes,' so I says, 'You must be one of them then, hey, mustn't you?' So we just left it at that like, didn't bother, and then she says, 'Ooh, why don't you ask the screw to move you in here,' like, because the girl that was in with her had got discharged that day, she wasn't a gay kind at all. So anyway, I says I'd think about it – I says, 'I'm getting a bit pissed off with the one upstairs anyrate,' I says, 'she's a bit of a drag like,' 'cause she wasn't a dyke either, if you know what I mean; you could sit and have a talk like. So I says, 'I'll let you know Friday anyrate,' and she says, 'Well, in the meantime,' she says, 'I'll tell the screw I don't want no one here, right.'

* You were moved in?
Yeah, all my things.

* The dyke mafia.
It is a dyke mafia in prison.

* So tell us about your relationship with this girl. What happened after you moved in?
Well, like I said, I moved in like, just – you're going to bloody laugh now, it'd be just like me, get myself – well I'd moved in, anyrate, so we were in bed together, not really doing nothing, just snogging, something like that, hadn't got into that heavy petting like, we didn't do that till a few nights after till we really found we liked one another. Then, oh my God, what should bloody happen just when we were in the bloody middle of snogging, fucking eye looking in the door like that. I turned around and says, 'Fucking kinky bastards,' I went. [*Laughter.*] I wouldn't have minded but I felt so embarrassed. So after this she shouted out as loud as she could, 'Get back into your own bunk.' [*Laughter.*] Well you know, well, naturally, the whole fucking wing heard it all, didn't they. The next thing I felt bloody ill, you know. Well what it was then, I says, 'I'm only talking like, I'm only sitting on the bottom.' 'Get back in your own bunk right.' I says, 'OK, don't have to let the whole fucking nick know,' you know what I mean. [*Laughter.*] Going on like that, keep giving them bloody ideas, you know what I mean and all this jazz.

* What's your general feeling about being locked up?

When I first moved in I felt frustrated, but who doesn't, like? Being cut off from society just like that. But after the first few weeks I just adapted myself to it. I thought, What can I do? It's not as if I'm going to be locked up for ever. And I thought, Well, it's all women anyway. I thought, Well, it's my scene going, I'm going to meet the right one. Anyway, like I said, I adapted myself to it like and accepted the fact that I was locked up like, and I'd broken the law, so I had to take my punishment.

* Did it make you feel different about what you had done to get in there in the first place?

No, not really.

* What effect does it have on women to be in Holloway?

I suppose it could depend on the mentality, I suppose. I mean if you're neurotic or highly strung, then it can have a bad effect, you know. But, you know, if you're calm and collected and all the rest of it, then it makes no difference, you just accept the fact that you've broken the law. But, like I says, I seen a lot of girls have bad effects through it. Just being locked up, you know, they've had to have tranquillizers and one thing and another to keep them on a steady level whilst they're in the nick.

* But you don't think it reforms them?
I think some of them it does, yeah, and others no, you know. I suppose you could say the same thing about me really, 'cause I've got nicked again since I've come out. But you don't do these things to go inside, you just do it, you know – 'cause you need bread. You gotta live, but you can't tell the courts that, they don't listen to that.

* Well, the law's not for poor people is it?
That's why I always get nicked, see?

* Well, how do you support yourself now, Janet?
What, support myself?

* Well how – well, you're on the social security aren't you? Do you find that's enough?
No! It's not enough.

* Can you get by on that?
No I can't. I find it very, very hard you know. I get pissed off with it some weeks you know. I feel like going out and doing something. Well, I think, is it worth it – getting caught?

* But on the other hand, you've got to eat, haven't you?
Yeah, it's true, but it's like you were saying, there's no other law for the poor, is there, whatsoever? But what I say, you can't tell the court this, that you've got to scrimp and scrape and feed your kids and all the rest of it, can you? They've got no time for that – you shouldn't break the law, it's wrong like, doing these things. Do you know what I mean?

* You should starve. I was going to ask you about the social security and everything, and how you feel about it, and the dole office, and whether you get any help from them.
No, I certainly don't.

* What about social workers and child welfare people and all that?
In the Borough of Brent they're not much good at all. A lot of people complain about them. I reckon they can't do much. Like, I had a bit of a big argument with them one day up in the social services office. I went up there – I'd not long come out of nick, mind you. I turned round and said, 'Well, look, I just can't manage on this money,' I says, 'I don't want to have to go out and steal

53

again,' I says, 'but I can see it coming to that,' I says. No one does this because – people only do it to get by, just in case you think people do it because they want to. It's not like that. So, anyway, she says, 'Let's look at the chart,' like, you know. In other words, look to see what you're entitled to, and she said, 'Well, this is what you are entitled to.' 'Yeah,' I says, 'this ain't no bloody good is it?' I says, 'I think I should get a lot more,' I says, like. 'Thousands of others like me, I'm not saying I'm the only one like, there must be thousands of others like me who just don't speak up, you know.' Anyway, she just went on and on, so I says to her, 'Oh, you're all the fucking same, you're all in the same boat, you know. You don't do nothing to help anyone. And if I get caught again you're going to say, why do I do this?' I says, 'What I tell you time and time again, I do these things because I need that bit extra, I just can't manage it.' I says, 'It's not as though I'm going to bingo or anything like that. That I'm blowing my money, 'cause I'm not. I smoke, admittedly, but I got to have some pleasure, you know.' I tried to make a point to her like, that someone has to have some pleasure.

* And she couldn't understand that?
Oh no, she couldn't understand it. A lot of people complain about the Brent Social Services, they're no good whatsoever.

* What sort of things do you do in your spare time, Janet, if you've got any?
Oh, I go visiting me mates, you know, or I go up the West End looking around in the big stores and that. Oh, I always find something to do. Or, sometimes I might just stay in and do a few things around the house, if I've let it go for weeks and weeks.

* What kind of dyke activities do you have?
Well there's none going on at the moment. There was one not so long ago.

* I didn't really mean affairs. I mean, what kind of dyke social things do you go to?
Oh, I go the Gateways, don't I? Go to Sappho.

* And that's all, those two? Have you ever had any contact with the Women's Movement?
No, I haven't.

* Have you any views on it, or haven't you really thought about it?

Well, I've never really looked into it, or gone out of me way to find out about it. It might be an idea, you know. I can always give it a try.

* Have you got any political views at all?
No, I haven't. I'm not really into anything politically, if you know what I mean.

* Have you ever voted?
No. I don't.

* Why not?
I just don't believe in it. I tend to think they're all the bloody same – once they get into power, that's it. Especially where the working class is concerned. The working class don't seem to get anything out of it. Now, look at the Labour Government. In the past they have been good, right, but this one's just fucking useless. People that have been thrown out of work going on the dole, you know, one thing and another.

Jackie Forster

Jackie Forster is fifty. She was born in London and went to Wycombe Abbey School. From 1945 to 1950 she was in repertory and from then she worked on TV and radio for the BBC where she met and married Peter McKenzie. They were divorced after three years. She appeared on 'Highlight' and 'Tonight', and also had her own programme. From 1958 to 1967 she appeared on TV in the United States and did lecture tours. She started Sappho *in 1972, and still continues to edit the magazine and run the meetings. At present she teaches drama in Ashford Prison.*

* *Sappho* magazine grew out of *Arena Three* didn't it? Was that the start of lesbian meetings and magazines?

Living with Babs my lover for many years and the kids we had this incredible set-up. Her godmother's housekeeper in the Lake District used to receive *Arena Three*. It came through our door in a brown envelope because of the children, and I opened one first for a change and saw this great appeal for press, because unless *Arena Three* is advertised we're just going out of existence. So I went creeping along to a meeting in a pub, shaking because I didn't know what I was going to look at because I'd never seen lesbians and I didn't know what they were going to look like. Anyway, I listened, and two weeks later there was another meeting, so I said to Babs, 'Let's go along.' We tried to get *Arena Three* advertised in the *Paddington Mercury*, but no hope. I was quite surprised. I didn't mind putting my name and address down. Then Babs chaired the meetings and they grew. Then Esme said, would I guest edit and help on the magazine, which was the first time I'd ever known how a magazine was put together. And that was back in 1969, *Arena Three* grew and the meetings grew. Then the hassle happened. We kept the meetings going – about fifteen of us. And they said we want another magazine and we said, 'Who? What? Where's the money?' And twelve brave ladies met over about six weeks, weekly meetings, drafting out what sort of magazine we wanted. I've still got the original document, and this was *Sappho*. They said we want these people still to do it, we want this kind of stuff going into it and this is probably why we've never changed the magazine from the original conception.

* Was that when you came out?
No, I came out in 1970. That's when I started 'speakers' corner' for CHE. But even though I came out, that was me, inside I still winced when people talked about dykes or lesbians, you know. *Oh God, I hope they don't find out it's me.* Now I go onto the attack, but not aggressively. I say, 'Why do you make that kind of comment?' And it didn't happen all of a piece, inside or politically.

* So you were 'out' publicly, but in your own personal, private life you didn't want people to know?
Only to lesbians, not to straight people. But well, I've never had a straight person ask me, 'Are you a lesbian?' you know, which is terribly awkward because it would be lovely to say, 'Yes.' I mean I'm finding I'm always saying, 'Are you gay?' and they say, 'No, I'm not,' and I say, 'Well, I am.' And I have to do it that way. So I'm pushing it all the time. And then sometimes they say, 'Yes I am gay,' but I didn't dare say it. But nobody has actually said, 'Are you a lesbian?' and given me that lovely moment of saying, 'Yes,' and putting them at their ease.

* When did you first have a lesbian affair?
When I was married – which was a stupid thing I did.

* What? Getting married?
Yes . . . no, I mean it was just this thing – these married women saying, 'Why aren't you married?' Married men never said, 'Why aren't you married?' Single women never said, 'Why aren't you married?' Single men never did. It was these married women who said, 'Why aren't you married?' It began to worry me and I thought, Golly, I ought to get married.

* How old were you?
Thirty-two and Peter was thirty-three. We'd had an affair for three years. We had our own bolt holes, and when we couldn't stand each other we pissed off and went out with other people.

* How long had you been married when you managed to get a divorce?
We had to wait the prescribed three years before we could get the divorce, but after eighteen months we were beginning to disintegrate.

* Had you begun to have affairs with women by then?
Oh no, nothing – I never knew. I was always attracted by lesbians – the idea of them – but I'd never met any. If someone said, 'She's a lesbian . . .' Ooooh! But I had none of this in me apart from schoolgirl crushes and best friend and this kind of thing. And, I mean, the heterosex scene was very good, I had a lot of lovers. I don't think I was promiscuous, but I liked men for different reasons. Total roleplaying character I was. Eventually I was at Lord's Cricket Ground for this luncheon, and this woman came in. I went 'cause everyone said Kay Kendall was coming but she didn't show up – so I thought I'd go too. We were the only two women, and she said, 'Come and spend Christmas,' because I was touring again in the States then.

* Did you go?
Peter came over and we went down and stayed with her. It was New Year's Eve night – I was tremendously influenced by her – she was an incredible, amazing real, driving American woman. On New Year's Eve for some unknown reason the turkey came flying through the door and her sister-in-law was shouting at her. She came in, in floods of tears, and I just held her and said, 'Whatever is going on?' and the next thing I knew we were kissing, and as far as I remember, as they drink a lot in the States, I went to bed with her that night and it was like something I'd never experienced in my life. Then it was very hairy because Peter was there too; and there was all this dodging about, and we went down to Florida. We went to Miami and we went down the Keys and over to the Bahamas.

* Were you in love? How were you feeling?
Aaah! I was just shaking, I was purple and cold. I had sweats and I kept fainting and all these things of the classic love sickness. And then to and fro across the Atlantic for three years, which was good because I always had these tours and she was on a paper in the States, so she was always in another place and I knew I just couldn't live with Peter. I couldn't tell him, I couldn't tell my parents, it was so astonishing. He said, 'Nobody must know, it will ruin you,' and I

really thought, This drama is going to show on my face, you know, I'll break out with these lesbian signs; and she was in the closet too. It was just terrible. I never even knew there was a gay scene, I'm not sure there was in '58.

* You thought you were the only lesbians in the whole world?
Absolutely – only two that this happened to – but of course she'd been on the scene a long time, but I was naïve, I didn't realize.

* Did you think of yourself as a lesbian then, or were you trying to pretend you were bisexual or what?
No, I thought, Oh God, I'm one of these lesbians.

* Were you frightened?
Horrified. I was absolutely appalled. What would happen to the family, what would happen to me and people finding out this awful thing? But I didn't know what awful thing I was, because apart from her who I adored, and she did adore me, I hadn't met any other lesbians that I knew about or saw. So it was this terrible myth, ignorance, social conditioning.

* When was that, in '58?
Nineteen fifty-eight to '61. Then my mother got cancer and I nursed her for six months. Then got my divorce and went over to the States and she met me with another woman. As we came in to land I could see them from the air and I knew. I said I don't want this plane to land. And sure enough, she moved on to somebody else, you know that was sickening and so I shook myself up very dramatically in the Biltmore Towers hotel and I sent myself a telegram from my agent saying, 'Date in New York, leave at once.' Then I spent ten days where it was the closest really I've come to suicide because there didn't seem to be any point in all that three years and being able to get it together. I mean, it was quite a heavy thing, and I suppose if we hadn't been in the closet and new – I mean, I could have handled it. Then I went back to the heterosexual scene and thoroughly enjoyed it, so I knew I wasn't a lesbian. It was just that I had, for the first time in my life, fallen in love with a woman – another woman who loved me.

* So how did you get back to women again?
I met this man in Canada and made a pass at him. This was Babs's husband. Then I met her, and after about six weeks I was madly in

love with her and I told her and she'd never had anything like this happen to her in her life. About two weeks later we kissed on the mouth, and about three months later we went to bed for the first time. We didn't know where the gay scene was. We tried to find it in New York. We found some filthy place – oh, it was awful – where we walked in dressed as straights, of course, because nobody must know, and sat at this table with some tapped beer. I had a different tongue in each ear, and I said, 'What's happening to you?' and she said, 'What's happening to you?' and then these diesels moved in and obviously were making for us. That was a great

shock and I said, 'Well, if that's the lesbian scene, I don't like it.' And Babs said the same thing, so we went back into the closet. Then again to and fro across the pond because she lived in Canada – that was for about two years. Then, amazingly enough, she decided she would come and live in England, and the children were going to be educated here and she was going to find me because I'd left and we would live together.

* And she found you? Were you surprised?

Astonished. I didn't even know she was in England. She suddenly arrived at the house one day. Eventually we moved in together, and it was really quite . . . I can say beautiful because we were both at the same stage and we both came out slowly together and into politics. We found, going at our own speed, we really found our way, and then I think one night, without really making a thing about it, we said (not so precisely) that as long as we lived, knowingly, we wouldn't let any other woman go through this idiot shit we'd been through because it was so perfectly ridiculous, and therefore let's do something about it. And just out of that tiny little comment so *Sappho* happened, and meetings, and into the real political scene. And coming out publicly and politically I had no hesitation now in tackling busybodies and politicians and whoever organized our lives in any areas to do with women and saying, 'Well, what about lesbians?'

* What was it like, Jackie, when you first came out?
A kind of relief, but I was still suspicious. But it wasn't until last year when I found my gay identity that I thoroughly knew that I loved women and not just one woman. I mean I really do love women. They hassle me to hell and I'm terrible to them and with them, but I do. And there wasn't any substitute for men, and a lot of it's to do with the Women's Movement, but I just knew this was exactly where I'd grow and where I wanted to be. And that released enormous energies.

* You said you came out in 1970, but it wasn't until last year that you discovered your real identity as a lesbian woman. That's an interval of five years. What was it that brought this about?
Well I was into CHE a lot and, being on the executive of CHE, gradually I realized however forceful I was or however much I was myself, the men, not consciously, forced a woman's role on me. And I started to get very restless and short with the male CHE members and then I got much more interested in the Women's Movement and Women in Media, which is the workshop I'm with, and being part of this Women's Rights Campaign. I was not allowed to be, you know, a feminist woman in CHE, which seemed to be the big scene, because they simply didn't know what feminism was about. But the Women's Movement knew what it was about and a lot of lesbians were beginning to get into this feeling that to be

a lesbian was to be political, and they were exploring it. And I just found I was having to put the brakes on in the male gay movement and I wasn't having to put brakes on with the straight women and I just knew my identity was with women. I mean, I don't exclude men, but I – they don't use my energies now.

* When your affair with Babs ended after nine years – how did it affect you?
I was, you know, much more free in finding myself relating to a lot of other women. And I was amazed that a lot of other women really cared about the state I was going through. I never thought they'd care, because I was this horrible, bossy person. And, I mean, to be able to be vulnerable and, you know, having to take because there was no other way – this was good, and I think that's what made me feel, Oh look, I don't always have to have the answers, I can just go and say, 'Oh shit, I'm in a terrible mess. Help.' And nobody said, 'Well, what sort of help do you want?' They just knew, but, I mean, this is marvellous to find out that lesbian women can do this. They don't say, 'Well, what would you like me to do?' They just knew, they just handled it and they carried me, and that's made me much less private and much more trusting. I'm just so mad that it's happened to me too late and I could have been like this in my thirties.

* What do you mean, too late?
Well it is a bit late because, you know, the gay men do treat me like a bit of a mum.

* Do gay women?
Quite a few do, quite a few do. I mean I'm just amazed when I'm just sitting there obviously looking boss-eyed into my glass and pissed and somebody comes up throbbing, saying, 'You're the only one who can help me.' And I find that instinctively I say, 'Well, what is it?' and all these troubles come trotting out. Well, I mean I would have thought anybody even half a mile away would think, Christ, don't go near her now she'll just go – you know, leave me alone, I'm having a trauma or something. But this has happened and I do listen. But I mean I never know what to say, because I don't know what the answers are, but somehow listening does help, and I'm quite amazed at the amount of people who trust me and, you know, say, 'You've been around a lot and know a lot and so

you should know.' And I think it quite shocks them when I say I haven't actually. I've only loved two women very much indeed, and that's about all my experience.

* If you were to embark on another very strong relationship with another woman . . .
I have. It's shattered me at my age, really. I'm fifty if you're interested.

* We were going to ask you that actually.
Somebody described it beautifully, menopausal urge! She said, 'We all go through it,' and I just yelled. And that brought it into perspective. It's very much this same feeling I had for Hattie who was my first love, of this force which just takes me over. It's not that I'm 'in love' – I'm absolutely insane, trying to find a phone to ring. I don't know what the hell I'm going to ring about. And then I spend hours saying, 'Don't pick up the phone.' And then I think no, and an idiot forty minutes go by saying, Look, don't bother her. But there is this thing which takes me over and I have to phone. I have to be in contact through sound if I can't be in physical contact. Now there were two or three men that I really loved, but not to this extent. It was absolutely acceptable that they would phone me, whereas if I phoned them they'd think I was chasing them. Therefore this was perfectly easy to resolve and I can't resolve this thing . . .

* Well, there are no guide-lines are there?
This is the thing, you see, making your own guide-lines. Now it bothers me in this sense, and that it's interfering with what I'm doing. I was just picking myself up and getting my head together and getting my space ordered and I was getting things done very quickly, and now what happens? I pick things up, I put things down, fifteen minutes go by and I don't know what the hell I've been doing. There's five minutes' concentration, then this thing comes on me again and the strongest thing I've ever had has been with women. Never the same equivalent with a man. I don't know, I suppose one bottles it up and goes and sails for Samarkand or some damn-fool thing.

* Would you want to have the same kind of relationship again as you had with Babs?
Oh no. Oh no no no. I mean it's going to take a hell of a lot to

move, you know, under the same roof. It really is – I mean I've made that perfectly clear. I don't think there's even a same roof context going on, or concept anyway, but I would never become exclusively involved, because I do think one or the other – I don't know which one it is – will mould you the way they want you. It's interesting, this is the first time I've been able to say, 'Oh God, I'm in love, I can't believe it, and I'm loved.' And this is a wonderful thing to say, just like it's an ordinary natural thing, and having the response back off people saying, 'How great.' This monogamy hassle . . . I still think vis-à-vis sex . . . I can only cope with one

woman at a time, but I'm totally capable and able to love more than one woman at a time. But I'm not sure . . .

* What's the difference, then? Why?
There are several women in *Sappho* who I love. We haven't been to bed together, but when they come in through the door it's the most beautiful thing. I put my arms around them, hear what they have to say in my ear and I can say it in theirs and this is absolutely sensual. But actually to physically be able to need and want two

women at the same time – I don't think I can. I think I am, when physically involved, monogamous. When I'm not physically involved and I love someone or several people, then I'm capable of going to bed, but it's not . . . I'm capable of having sex . . . it's not something that's going to turn into a relationship. I mean I usually make that pretty clear, 'Well, darling, if you want to find out about it . . . but I'm not going to marry you.' It's amazing too in *Sappho* the amount of women who come in and say, 'Well, I've never . . . could I with you?' Like you've been around, you know everything – and I'm amazed. Well, they think that's a great compliment, but my God, I'm not going to knock them off for one night so they can find out what lesbianism is about. I mean it may be a dreadful experience for them.

* It isn't a very good way of finding out, is it?
No, and then, you know, I go into this whole thing: it must be caring for women, loving women and finding friends and then boom the one you like. Well, that's not true, I have certainly in the last year, I've had sex for its own sake, and it was just like having it with a man and so isolated at the end of it because there was no emotional thing taking over.

* Why do you think this happened? How do you think you got into that situation?
Mainly because I was lonely and I hadn't had sex for such a long time and it was there and I thought, Why not? I mean I wasn't drunk to do it or anything else, it was very mechanical. I couldn't get over it, you know – somehow we just stayed apart.

* It doesn't lift off?
Exactly, and it's the not lifting off that I don't think is worth it. I mean you have to find out, but I wasn't looking for it, it just happened. But I thought, God Almighty, this is just like the times you sleep with men, that 'no lift off' is exactly the phrase.

* But a certain amount of one-night stands always go on . . .
That's why I've always loved *Sappho* actually, because it isn't a bar scene – I mean, there's such a lot of dialogue going on between groups of women, couples of women all over the room, and you can actually find out about people instead of, you know, crashing music, dim lights, alcohol haze . . .

Gerry Allen-Manson

Gerry Allen-Manson is twenty-one. She is a music student at Exeter University. She is president of the University GaySoc and a member of her local CHE group.

* Perhaps we should ask Gerry a bit about her family background . . . no, perhaps we should ask her . . . do your parents know you're gay?

Yes . . . but I think it's quite important to fit me into my family background . . . My father died when I was four months old and my mother married again when I was about one and a half, and that was a very unhappy marriage. She was separated from my stepfather when I was seven, and finally divorced when I was eleven, and I was always sheltered from that, so that when I look back on my childhood I feel that I was quite a happy child, just like any child. There was an absence of men around. She did finally remarry – she went out to work full time and she was very lonely . . . she used to come home and do the housework and so on. She always used to say she tried to be a mother and father to me to make up for me not having a father. Her friends at work used to say, 'You ought to go out more and meet someone,' and she finally did. They got her to join a Marriage and Friendship Bureau, and through that she met someone she really got on with and they finally got married when I was about sixteen.

* How did you feel about that?

Well, I was happy for my mother because I didn't like to think of her being on her own. I was very happy that she'd found someone, and I got on well with my stepfather – but he immediately felt that he ought to assume the role of the father figure and be strict and tell me what to do, and by the age of sixteen you don't want someone to tell you what to do. Well, it was difficult, we did have slight problems at first, but we all get on very well now. At that time I started to worry about being gay and feeling that I didn't fit in with my friends at school.

69

* What sort of school did you go to?
A girls' grammar school.

* And what were your feelings then towards women?
Well, by the time I was about eleven or twelve I started having crushes on women, usually girls that were older than me at school, and occasionally teachers, and it started getting really intense. I'd always been rather a tomboy at school, I suppose – you know, climbing trees and fishing – and I've never been pushed into being ladylike when I was little. I didn't use to like playing with dolls – I'd rather play with train sets and I used to get kidded about this. I suppose by the time I left junior school I did feel that I was different in some way. I couldn't pin down what it was.

* What about when you were sixteen, because that's the age when the crush period is supposed to end and you're supposed to take a healthy heterosexual interest in boys?
When I was twelve I had a crush on this girl at school – I hadn't told her – she was four years older than I was – I sort of worshipped her from afar. I had boy-friends from the age of thirteen. When all my friends started going out with boys, I did as well.

* Did you feel they put you under pressure to do that?
No, I don't think so – exploration really, the same as most of my friends, because it never occurred to me that I could be gay. I probably had more boy-friends than my friends did, even when I was sixteen. By then I'd started wondering if I was gay. I knew what the word lesbian meant by then, and it was my sort of secret worry, and it was something that I didn't dare mention to anybody because I felt it was abnormal and freakish. I'd never met anybody that openly said they were gay; but by then I'd admitted to myself that that's what I was – I thought I wouldn't change, I felt too intensely.

* Were you frightened?
Yes, I was very frightened.

* Did you continue to go out with boys then?
Yes, I did. I suppose mostly because boys knew me and they wanted me to go out with them, and I just didn't like to say no because I didn't like them to think that I didn't like them 'cos I got on very well with boys.

* Were you attracted to them?
No, I wasn't, and it was a great problem, and I didn't know how to cope with it. I felt affectionate towards them, and that was all really, but if they got any more serious than that I used to make excuses, wanting to go home early and things like that. I also had a crush on a girl who was at school with me, who I saw every day because she did the same 'A' levels I did.

* Had you had any relationships with women at that stage?
No, I hadn't – I'd always been much too scared to start anything – I mean at school it was all sort of, 'What did you do? Who did you go out with last night?' I became very introverted because I bottled it up . . . I thought, I can't be . . . someone like me can't be a lesbian . . . I like men too much to be gay . . . But then I thought, Well, it doesn't necessarily mean you hate men. So in the end I found out through *Woman's Own*, I saw someone had written in saying they were worried because they thought they were gay, and Marjorie Proops or whoever it was told them an address they could write to, so I wrote off to this address – it might have been CHE – and they put me in touch with *Arena Three*. So I wrote to ask for a subscription to the magazine, and I found it catered for women who had come to terms with themselves that were into the gay scene, and I couldn't really identify with that so I felt I couldn't really reach anybody . . . I looked at the ads though – I desperately wanted to meet someone.

* How old were you then?
Seventeen or eighteen. I was in my last year at school, and the people that put the advertisements in were mainly thirties and forties. So I just read as much as I could and tried to educate myself. I got books on homosexuality – anything I could get hold of. I really felt seriously that I was gay and tried to accept myself.

* The girl you were attracted to at school – did you talk to her?
No. I never did. I think she might have realized. She definitely wasn't gay though. She was fond of me. I did show her I was fond of her, and she didn't mind, but if she had realized how attracted I was – if she'd known it was physical as well, she'd have been quite repulsed I think – so I never did tell her. I used to go to school thinking, Now shall I tell her today? When I was on my own with her in rehearsals and things I used to say to myself, Tell her . . . go

on! I never got round to it. It got so frustrating – in the end I almost stopped myself from seeing her because it was so frustrating. But I talked myself out of it – I kept saying to myself, She won't feel the same as you. It's quite pointless. When I came down to Exeter I was worried about how I was going to fit into university. I thought, Well, all my friends will be trying to introduce me to men because I haven't got a boy-friend, and I'm going to have to tell people. Luckily, in the first year, I had a room-mate who I was at school with. The very first night we were sharing a room, she was telling me about her boy-friend and she was saying, 'If we're going to be room-mates, I don't think we ought to have any secrets.' She was telling me all about her boy-friend, so in the end I said, 'Well, Janet, if we're not going to have any secrets perhaps I ought to tell you something'; and I told her all about how I felt towards women and she was very shocked – it had never dawned on her – she'd never thought about anything like that before. But she was very understanding. It started off being a secret between us because I felt I still couldn't be myself with all the other girls in my hall. I was in a single-sex hall of residence, and they were always talking about boy-friends and love and things, and I felt I couldn't be myself unless I told them how I felt. Because there was a GaySoc in the university, that it made it even more tense – I kept thinking, Perhaps I ought to join, and at the same time I thought, Perhaps I am too young to make my mind up. Well, I suppose I was afraid really of losing the friends I'd made so far – that I'd be rejected if they knew I was gay – it would be so alien to them. Of course, I'd told my mother during the summer . . .

* What did she say?
She still thought it was a phase. She was angry – well – hurt rather. She was hurt that I hadn't told her before. She said it was nothing to be worried about, and that I would grow out of it. She said, 'Keep an open mind and try and meet as many people as you can while you're at university, and don't make mountains out of molehills – I'm sure you're not gay.' She said she used to have a friend at school who she was very close to and friends used to call them lesbians, but there was no physical attraction there. So I said, 'Well, there is physical attraction as far as I'm concerned.'

* And how does she feel about it now?

Well, she started to understand – she started to be really under-standing about it. She told my stepfather, and he tried to be understanding and they tried to help me as much as they could. They wanted me to be happy. They felt that if I was gay, then, OK, they'd stand by me . . . But recently, just since April, they've started to talk to Jehovah's Witnesses and they've become involved in this now. I don't know why – probably because Jehovah's Witnesses seem to have an answer for everything and they seem to be the sort of people who need an answer for everything.

* Has it changed your relationship with them at all?
Yes, it has. It was awful over the summer because they talked to this Jehovah's Witness . . . and they asked him about homo-sexuality, but he didn't know very much about the subject, so he read up about it and did some research – and came back and told them all the references in the Bible, which he said he takes literally, and he said it's an abomination against mankind and it's a mishap which occurs in evolution, and it's not natural and all sex should be to procreate . . . it's all very fundamental, and my parents now feel that the state of homosexuality isn't wrong but the practice of it is.

* Have you come to terms with your homosexuality now?
I have, yes.

* How did that come about?
Just by thinking and thinking and talking to people . . . going into religion and philosophy and more and more self-analysis.

* Have you had many relationships with women?
Well – by the time I was in the first year I still hadn't really had any relationships with other women, but I felt that the attraction was there in me – I was sure that I was gay, and I really did feel isolated. I really wanted to meet someone who felt the same as me. And even after joining GaySoc – there weren't any women – it made me feel even more isolated; it made me feel a freak, you know – why should I be the only woman in three and a half thousand students who was gay? Why should I be the only one who had come out and been open about it? I didn't even know that *Gay News* existed, but one of the blokes at GaySoc who does music with me told me about *Gay News* – he gave me a copy, and in the end I wrote an ad in it and said I'd like to meet somebody to talk to or write to someone

that felt the same as me. I got four replies – I described myself as a 'femme' student.

* What happened – what was the result?

I met one girl who was at a public school in Bristol who was very politically conscious and we didn't really hit it off. We didn't really talk to each other very well – I was only in Bristol for one day anyway – and we just never got to know each other – she was quite nice, though. There was one girl who was a secretary in Leicester, but she was living with her auntie and she said, 'Only write to me on Fridays because my auntie collects all my letters the rest of the week and reads them, and if they're from anybody who's gay she burns them'; and I thought, Crikey – what a set-up – who on earth would want to get involved in something like that! Another one was twenty-seven – she was a taxi-driver in Bournemouth – I didn't get around to writing to her, and the other girl, Vivien, was a student teacher, and she seemed to have the most in common with me. She didn't seem to be worried at all about how she felt, but said that women friends that she was attracted to – after she told them how she felt – regarded her with a noticeable reserve as if she was going to strip off any minute and rape them. But we got writing. She'd come to terms with herself – probably because she didn't identify herself as totally gay – she could fit into society and go out with blokes and so on – until she fell in love with a girl who was a bit younger than her, and whose mother was a Jehovah's Witness and forbade any further contact once she found out about them and their relationship. In the end we met, and we really hit it off straight away, but she lives in London so I don't see her very often.

* So you started having an affair with her?

Yes.

* She was your first sexual experience?

Yes – yes, apart from a girl in Birmingham, but I can't really call that an affair because we only saw each other about three times, but I was attracted to her.

* Did you get off with her?

Yes – well, sort of. [*Laughter*.] Well, we slept together, but – you know – we didn't go very far . . .

* Were you frightened?

She was frightened – I suppose I was as well. Yes. Yes, I was a bit.

74

We were both a bit drunk as well, we'd just been to a party – both a bit tipsy.

* Did you think you weren't going to know what to do?
Yes – well, I always felt that I ought to be in love with someone before I felt, well, you know. I had the conventional ideas about being in love with someone before you give yourself totally to them – so I didn't really know how I felt towards this girl in Birmingham.

* Have you had an affair with anyone on campus?
No, not really, not as such. I have been attracted to several girls, but they're all straight. Just recently this term I fell for a girl and told her how I felt – she knew I was gay before, I'd always been quite open about it. She's been really nice about it. We still see each other and go out together.

* Don't you feel frustrated being on campus surrounded by three and a half thousand so-called heterosexuals. I mean, obviously some of them must be homosexual, but you're the only one you know of, aren't you?
Yes, very. Well, there is a first-year, but she seems to be very uptight about how she feels. I've heard she's gay, but I haven't actually met her.

* Well, tell us how you feel in this situation.
A bit difficult, really. I often feel alienated – that I don't fit into society. Luckily I've got really close friendships with some gay blokes in the university.

* Is that an adequate substitute, though?
Well, not entirely, no. I'm reasonably happy and I don't want to settle down at the moment – Vivien knows that. I mean she was quite possessive with me, but we've talked about possessive relationships and monogamy and we've decided we don't really want to be possessive at the moment, till we really know how we feel – but we're too young to settle down, she's only a year older than me.

* And you haven't really met any gay women yet, have you?
No, so we both sort of live our own lives – but if only people weren't so uptight about it. I mean, there must be more gay women in the university – they must be very repressed as well.

* There must be hundreds.
It's supposed to be one in ten, one in fifteen.

* It started off as one in twenty, that's what Kinsey said, but it seems to have scaled down.
I often wonder, though, why women are repressed, why they don't come forward and say they're gay.

* Have you had any sexual relationships with men?
Yes, well, boy-friends I went out with.

* How did you feel about that? Did you get anything out of it?
Not really, not emotionally. Because I wasn't attracted to them.

* What about physically?
No – well, I can reach a climax with a man, but I still felt emotionally void really – emotionally unfulfilled.

* In what way?
Because I wasn't attracted emotionally I didn't feel that I loved them emotionally – there was just something lacking, I couldn't pinpoint it. Just the softness and sensitivity and gentleness and tenderness of a woman.

76

* I was going to ask you why you are physically and emotionally attracted to women?
I just find that women are more graceful and gentle and sensitive, and that's what I'm attracted to.

* Could men be like that?
If they hadn't been brainwashed to put on this toughness I suppose, but I think women are more naturally sensitive and gentle – perhaps because they have children and bring them up.

* Have you ever thought you were a bisexual?
Well, I thought that seeing as I got on well with men, and I could go to bed with a man quite happily, that maybe I am bisexual, but I always feel there's something lacking with men. I've never been really strongly attracted to a man – I can find them attractive, but there isn't the same emotional attraction that I find with a woman.

* You're out of the closet at university here, aren't you?
Yes.

* What sort of reaction have you had from the other students?
They tend to feel sorry for me, I think, because they feel that it's normal to be heterosexual, to get married and have children, and that I won't have that; but then they realize that I don't feel sorry for myself. I would like to have children, but I wouldn't like to get married. I do feel pressurized by my parents – they'd like to have grandchildren, and they'd like me to get married because they did. They don't really understand it.

* How do you see your future as a gay woman musician? What ambitions do you have?
I certainly think my career will be very important . . . I can't see myself living with one person, in an exclusive relationship – I'd rather see myself relating to other people on lots of different levels – both men and women, but not men on a sexual level.

* So you don't want to get married to a woman and settle down, so to speak?
Perhaps that's what I want to do, perhaps I haven't met the right woman yet. I could imagine myself falling in love and feeling that I'd rather be with her than anyone else. At the moment, going on my previous experiences, I just like to meet as many people as

77

possible, and have a circle of close friends who understand me, and who I can be myself with.

* Is sex very important to you?
Yes, I suppose it is really, but I think the emotions behind that are more important. I don't feel that it's a great strain for me if someone doesn't feel sexually attracted as long as they like me personally, and don't mind me being affectionate towards them – I don't feel that the actual sex act is of primary importance.

* Would you like to be part of a lesbian social scene?
At the moment, the lesbians I've met in Exeter are very tense – well, I'm generalizing, I suppose – but they're either afraid of you getting to like them too much, and they don't want their partner to be jealous, or else they want to go out with you and daren't ask because they think you're not interested.

* What about women's groups – do you know of any?
One just started a week ago – I'm going to join next term, make my presence known. I'm sure there'll probably be some gay women there, and we can have a talk between GaySoc and Women's Rights. They're both working towards liberation and trying to find out your sexual identity, being honest with yourself and not fitting into stereotypes.

* Is GaySoc working towards alleviating the oppression of women?
It's so male-dominated I feel overwhelmed – I tried to talk about women's rights and got shouted down by the men. They felt that because lesbians don't have any legal things against them that there is complete toleration for women – that because women haven't come to GaySoc it was because they were having their relationships OK, they didn't feel oppressed and therefore they didn't feel the need to come, which is totally ridiculous, and I tried to say so, but none of them were interested.

* Why don't women come to GaySoc, then?
Because, I think, they are more oppressed. They probably think it's male-dominated, which it is, and instead of coming along to meetings and making their presence felt . . . I think it's partly apathy, and in a way they're too afraid to come along. I'm going to try and get some leaflets printed next term specially for women and distribute them to all the women in the university – if the two male secretaries agree, because they control the money.

78

* Why did you decide to come out of the closet? In your life ahead you're going to have to fight quite a few battles through being out of the closet – because not everyone is as tolerant as they are in university. Why did you decide to take the risk and even be in a book like this?

Because I've been brought up to be open and honest about how I feel, and I couldn't see why people were so uptight about it. Also it just came gradually, really. I was afraid when I first joined GaySoc. I felt that I was leading a double life because I hadn't told most of my friends I was gay, and I was going along to gay meetings. And as

soon as I talked to people who were gay, I felt, well, what are we worried about? This is how I feel, and I should be honest and open about it. I can't live my life as a lie, it's hypocritical, you've got to say how you feel – I thought the more people who are honest about how they feel, the more people who are in the closet would feel that they could be honest, too. Then it would gradually become realized how many gay people there are, and it is a perfectly natural thing to be, how widespread it is. Then there'd be no reason to be frightened.

79

Gillian Love-Taylor

*Gillian Love-Taylor, known to her friends as
Taylor, is thirty-four. She was born in Barnet,
Hertfordshire, and went to Queen Elizabeth's
Girls' Grammar School, Barnet. She took a
degree in English at Reading University and later
qualified as a librarian. She got married at
twenty-two and was divorced after seven and a
half years. She became involved in the Women's
Movement around the time of her separation from
her husband and came out as a lesbian six months
later. At present she lives in London and works as
a bookseller.*

* When did you join CHE?
As soon as I got out of London I joined it because I felt I wanted to
belong to some big group. This was in Farnham. There were no
women's groups, no gay groups. The nearest gay group was in
Reading or Guildford.

* How long did you live there?
For four months last year. That was when I moved out of London
to live a healthy, quieter life.

* What happened?
My romance with Anna broke up and I came running back to
London in a flap and had a nervous breakdown and gave in my
notice.

* How did your nervous breakdown manifest itself?
Well in a minor way, not like you water signs – I took to drink.
Well, not really, there was one night when I had drunk a whole
bottle of wine and I was quite pissed. I couldn't get to the Ladies
easily. I even smoked cigarettes for a month! I didn't take up meat,
however. Oh, and lots of frenetic activity, joining *Sappho* and
meeting all you lovely ladies. Put myself about a bit.

* Were you really in love with her?

81

I have a funny idea about being in love. I think it is an escape from being ourselves in a way. I enjoy it when I'm in it. I do think it's a self-delusion. And what I actually think happened to me then was that I had been a very uptight self-repressed Virgoan person. I must have been, to stick in a marriage for seven and a half years. And then leaving London, leaving my flat, moving to Farnham, finding my own flat, my own job, I suddenly realized that this was the first time I hadn't done anything under the auspices of my parents or my husband. And I thought, Christ, this has happened fairly late in life.

* What do you think about falling in love? (She hates me asking questions like this!)
Well, I think it's very exciting and heady. In a way it's very danger-ous because you're carried away. But for the way I function it's not really what life is all about. For the past six years all my energies had gone into love relationships and I'd just been at the mercy of my emotions and that was something I had needed to go through as a growing process. But I felt that I was coming to the end of that and did need to control and not just be led astray like rushing back to London just because my romance had broken up. I should have had enough strength in myself to say, 'Fuck that, I want to be here and doing these things and never mind whether she's here or not.' Also, this was the first time that I had been a completely isolated homo-sexual. You know, I'd come out when I was in London and already in the Women's Movement, which is obviously more supportive, and I suddenly realized what a lot of people living in the provinces must go through and there just isn't another person you can talk to. Even, you know, those who will tolerate it, or tolerate you as an individual being homosexual. There was no one I could say to, 'Look, I'm really freaked out and I'm having a nervous breakdown because my lover's left me and she's a woman, and I can't tell anyone about it' – and I just was, I was saying to them, 'I'm having a lot of emotional difficulties,' but that's all you know.

* Who made you a vegetarian . . . your parents?
No, I gave up men and meat at the same time, meat slightly before men actually. George and I stopped sleeping together six months before we actually separated – which meant that our relationship vastly improved immediately because all the tension went out of it

82

and we were just good friends. And then I changed to being a vegetarian before he'd actually left, and I also changed my name before he left because I was changing my whole identity.

* Why did you get into that?

Mmmm, I knew, I mean, I had been very scornful of vegetarians – well, not exactly scornful, but I'd just . . . I was one of those very autocratic people who said the lower species are here for our use and we need meat, so we should kill them and eat it, and then I knew of some other vegetarians and so I suppose I thought a bit about it . . . but what actually made me change at that moment was

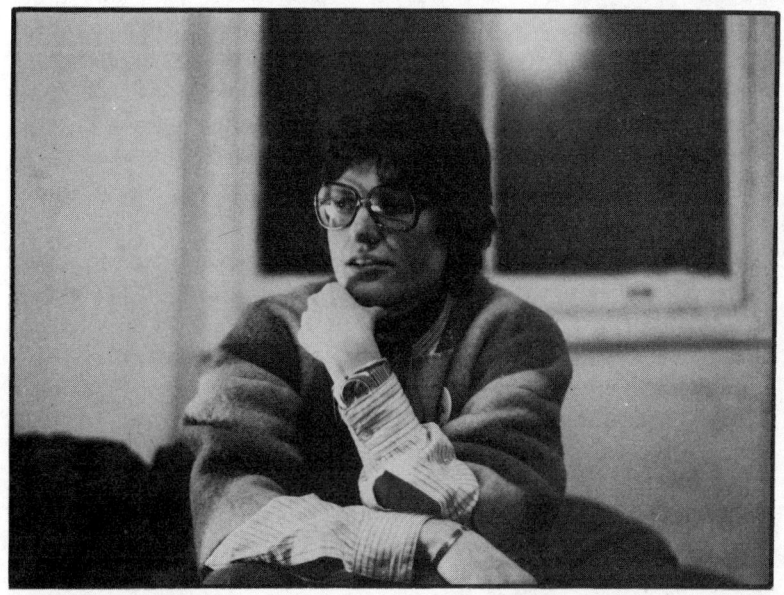

reading a biography of Bernard Shaw who, as you know, was a vegetarian, and I suppose it's always when you've got a concrete example that you think, I can do it too, and the particular thing – the reason why people sometimes have difficulty in changing is because they don't know what they can eat instead, and this particular book had a lot of menus in the back, so I mean, you know . . .

* What was the reason for it? That you think it's wrong to kill animals for food?

I think it's . . . it was a lot of reasons – it was the political reason that, you know, the West, we're living off protein which is got much more expensively by converting it into meat, and, in fact, in America certainly, and probably over here too, they eat too much protein, because they eat so much steak. We are living at a rate that is starving other people in other parts of the world.

* Do you reckon there's any relationship between feminism and vegetarianism? In the matriarchal societies they were all vegetarian, weren't they?

Mmmm . . . another reason why I changed is also because I think it's basically a more healthy diet, and that it's spiritually more healthy, because I think that when you eat animals, you're not only conniving with violence, you're consuming violence, and there is also the kind of scientific or technical thing that the animals know they're going to die and so they have all the adrenalin going through them, and then you eat meat and you get that and that makes you awful – you get their adrenalin as well . . .

* Really, is that true?

Yes, I mean, that's why meat eaters are aggressive, because they've consumed all those extra chemicals – but I do think that I'm more into – now – the kind of spiritual side of it than I ever was – the kind of mystical side of seeing life as a whole; and the reason I think it links with feminism is because I think that women are more humane and able to see these connections than men are, and that particularly now, women are the sort of last repositories of any humanity that remains in humans – and you know – we've been forced into a nurturing role and into looking after people rather than things, but that's a good thing . . . Things – you know, nations, armies, structures, multinational companies, or petrol pumps – and that sort of aspect of looking, of being sensitive to taking care of others, which men seem to have lost completely. I mean, I think it's possible for them to develop much more of it than they have – just as I think women need to develop a bit more drive than they have . . .

* How can they develop drive if they haven't got all that nice meat adrenalin running round in their bodies?

Well, anyone can call on the drive that's within them when they want to. I think that men or the great patriarchal society has fragmented and broken everything up into separate compartments in a way that women are not so likely to do – so that's how we can alienate ourselves from animals and so we can kill them and eat them – we can alienate ourselves from other people and put them to work in factories or we can alienate ourselves from our wives and mothers and make them work for us in the home or whatever – and that women don't see that because they see the individual person, or they're more able to. I think the SCUM Manifesto is quite mad in some ways because it's so extreme, but it takes extremists like that to often see right through things and, you know, it seems to be true, certainly at the moment, that men have such minute egos that everything they've built up is to boost their ego and everything they've done to other people and to themselves is continually this ego-boosting machine which the whole world has become to blow up the male ego . . . inflate, I mean.

* United States' imperialism being the prime example.
Yes.

* Is vegetarian food boring?
No, much more interesting than meat. You have to devote more thought to it – you have to devote more thought to the balance of your diet – I mean, meat eaters should devote more thought than they do, but it's very easy when you're a meat eater to go out and get chops and two veg or whatever, and particularly to buy convenience vegetables, frozen stuff. Mmmm, if you're a vegetarian you have to think about balancing your diet much more. You also have to think about not overcooking it, or it would be unpalatable, and meat eaters tend to go in for much stronger sauces and things. There's so much more variety in vegetables and fruits than there is in meat – even aesthetically . . .

* Tell us about when you started being interested in astrology.
There again, as with vegetarianism, I was very sceptical about astrology, and I also felt very oppressed by being a Virgo because it's one of the signs against which people are prejudiced. It was sparked off by the break-up with Anna because someone said to me, 'Oh, you're a Virgo and she's Aquarius, that's incompatible,' and Anna went off with a Libra and they said, 'Sorry, you've lost out on that,' and I said, 'Rubbish,' blah, blah, and then I went and read it up and a lot of what it said in fact was true and so – also,

85

as I'm very analytical, the character analysis appeals to me particularly . . .

* You're not into the prophecy? Kind of – 'Your week by the Stars'?
No, particularly not what you read in the newspapers, and I certainly started by reading very popular and quite banal sorts of astrology. Linda Goodman is a good introduction, but she's very popularizing.

* Why do you think dykes are so interested in astrology?
Because I think it's another of the ancient arts and/or sciences which women knew, which the matriarchy knew, I mean this sort of instinctive art which we had and that it is definitely a female science.

* Whenever you meet a dyke, they ask what star sign you are, even the ones who pretend they aren't into it . . .
Yes . . . but it . . . I mean the revival and interest in astrology and herbal medicine and diet are all forms of alternative knowledge or ancient knowledge which the technological age tried hard to stamp out.

* The patriarchal society . . .
Yes – and which culminated in the twentieth century and reached its absolute zenith beginning with the Industrial Revolution – and the whole thing with the growth of the power of women now and . . . I think that men too can call on those sort of powers, but they've just lost so much more touch with them than women have – I mean, obviously there are male astrologers and so on, who are perhaps much more gentle and humane people than the general run of male would be. The problem with astrology is that it's hetero-sexually oriented, of course – there's a dire need at the moment for a lesbian astrologer, I mean a book . . .

* Why don't you write it?
Well, I would like to when I know enough about it.

* It would be a mass bestseller. I don't know why someone hasn't done it. Is there a dykey star sign? Which star sign is the dykiest?
Mmmm, well the heterosexual astrologers say, 'Pick out various signs which are most likely to be bisexual and/or homosexual . . .' Gemini, of course. Aquarius is always known as being a progressive sign. Aquarian women are always described as likely to be interested in politics and particularly the Women's Movement at this time in

history, and very likely to be lesbians, but I would really like to do a survey and find out.

* Well, what is the most highly sexed sign then?
Scorpio. There are certainly a lot of homosexual Scorpios about, men and women.

* Well, what is your favourite sign? Which sign are you most attracted to?
Well, I try not to have a favourite sign, I don't think one should prejudice oneself against other signs.

* Oh, what a liberal answer!

But there are signs that I respond to personally more easily than others.

* Which star sign have you had the most lovers from?
Aquarius and Leo – absolutely fatal, I shouldn't have. I can often have affairs with both, but I always get too involved with them, which is silly, and in fact I relate in the long term much better to water signs or other earth signs, with whom I haven't had any relationships; but water signs, although very difficult, are

much more successful in the long run – even my husband.
* What's he?
Cancer.

* Good old Cancers.
I have heard from other people who know much more about astrology than I do, and I suspected this for myself that homosexuality can – you know you can't definitely say anything from a person's birth chart, you can only say 'has a tendency to' or 'comes under the influence', and it's up to the individual whether they strengthen or mitigate the qualities within themselves – but it can be seen that a person has a tendency to be a homosexual from their birth chart, and I think that's another survey that should be done.

* You should be the world expert on astrology – it would be so wonderful.
Well, I'm working at it, but it does take years of study – I mean, I started with very popular stuff and now I've got into more serious and complex things.

* You have to be quite good at maths, too, don't you?
But I'm not, so I'd have to get somebody else to do it – I'm only good at the kind of analytical and intuitive side of it.

* Do you believe in calculators?
The astrologer of the age of Aquarius with pocket calculator!

* Is it still the age of Aquarius?
We've only just come into it.

* What was it before?
Pisces.

* So it won't be Cancer till after I'm dead?
No, an age lasts at least 2,000 years! [*Laughter.*] Actually Leo will have as much influence in the Age of Aquarius, because Leo is the polarity of Aquarius.

* During the matriarchy, what age was it then?
We don't know, because the ages that are recorded begin with recorded history which is the patriarchal society, and the matriarchy has been written out, hasn't it?

Monica Sjöö

Monica Sjöö is thirty-seven. She was born in Sweden. She has three sons and at present lives in Bristol, where she paints, writes and is active in local women's groups. She has had several exhibitions of her paintings and prints and has published several articles.

* What was your family background? Did you live in Stockholm – or were you born there?

No. My mother was from the north, a drop-out from a middle-class family. My father came from the very opposite background, he was one out of ten kids from a peasant family from the south of Sweden. People from the north and south are very different from each other. He had taken himself through art school by painting kitchens.

* He was a painter too?

Yes. They met at the Art Academy in Stockholm, they went through art school for about six years together, sort of being comrades and painting together. Finally she married him and she was denounced by the family because he was lower-class and they treated my father really – I mean really like shit – even down to the thing of trying to teach him table manners. Her parents threatened her – don't you dare to get pregnant as well as marrying this terrible guy – and of course she did, accidentally, and she was so fearful – she didn't even let them know. She went along to the abortionist and was standing outside the door, and then she couldn't go through with it.

* This was you?

This was me. [*Laughter.*] They were not living in any way that they could have children (their love was painting) and they had no money, so having a child at that point was a disaster. All the time she was pregnant, they were travelling around having exhibitions all over the north of Sweden, living in a very unhealthy way. After I was born we moved down to the south of Sweden where my father came from. Then we lived in an attic, they didn't have hot water, a kitchen, any cooking facilities, a bath, nothing. You can imagine trying to bring up a baby when you can't even make some food. So they went out to eat and brought back ready-cooked food for me from a cheap little restaurant. She left him when I was three. She didn't like the people in south Sweden either, the whole way of living down there, she just couldn't get used to it.

* It's amazing that difference in such a small country.
The soil is very poor and very stony and the people have a very hard time to make a living out of the fields. All the fences are made of those big stones that have been dug up out of the earth. In the beginning of the century there was huge migration, particularly from that part of Sweden, to America. Before my father was born three of his oldest brothers had already migrated to America.

* How was your life then – just the two of you?
We went up to the north because her parents still lived there. She and me lived in a tiny little flat and she tried to make a living selling paintings, doing portraits.

* What effect did such an unconventional upbringing have in a conventional society like Sweden?
Well it was all right as long as we were in the north because it was small, provincial, people were kind, she knew a lot of people as her parents had lived there a long time. She had this fantasy about moving to Stockholm because she thought it would be better for her art, her work, contact with other artists or whatever. We moved there when I was eight. It was the worst mistake she ever made in her life 'cos we moved into this one room and kitchen in a block of flats on the outskirts of Stockholm, in a terrible place. For the next eight years she was completely isolated.

* And you as well?
Yes. When I grew up in Sweden there was this thing about conformity, everybody had to look the same, have the same things, dress the same. My mother was very eccentric, people used to think that she was a gipsy, she was taller than me, also she had long hair and very colourful clothes, really staggering. You could never not notice her.

* Were you ashamed or embarrassed by her?
No, not ever, she was my best friend, I completely identified with

her. And I was in many ways the only friend she had. At that age, six, seven, eight, she used to tell me everything, confide in me in every way. At the age of six or seven I was in the position of having always to protect her, which was very heavy. She was fearful of the people who lived around that place who disapproved of her. Children were not allowed to come and play at our place, I was completely isolated for years, but I never blamed her.

* Did she ever put any heterosexual pressures – or expectations of marriage, etc., on you?
No, she never did at all. She detested that whole female thing herself.

* She was a feminist?
I think you could say so, but not consciously. She was an anarchist, a born anarchist. She hated anything institutional, impersonal.

* So when you were at school, what you were taught there presumably was in conflict with your life at home?
I used to stay away from school half the terms, I hated schools. The whole problem was coming from the north of Sweden where I was a country girl with a thick northern accent, long plaits and kind of old-fashioned, dumped on the outskirts of Stockholm with big gangs of kids, huge schools with over forty in each class. I hated every minute of those four years. It was terrible and no friendliness. In the north everybody used to say hello, like each other and be concerned about each other – in Stockholm you could fucking die in the street and nobody would care less. I used to be taken the piss out of because of my northern accent, my plaits. The only thing that saved me was that I was always bigger than all the other girls and boys of my age – nobody sat on me in that way, they just tried to trample me psychologically and emotionally.

* When did you first start to paint? Did you always want to be a painter?
Well, my mother always used to say don't become an artist because it's just misery and poverty – and never marry another artist.

* So how did you get to be an artist?
The whole situation in Sweden is that there is a lot of art schools but they are all private and you have to pay to go there and there was no way I could get the money together. So for about two or

three years I worked as an artist's model, nude model, in the art schools. That was the only training I had in art.

* Were you painting at this time?
Not really. I knew when I left school at sixteen that that's what I wanted to do, but it took me about three years, bumming around Sweden and Europe before I could get enough security . . . you see, when I left home I was so depressed, I couldn't talk to anyone, I couldn't smile. Five years of my stepfather digging at me the whole time – we used to have terrible scenes – he was drunk all the time. He was jealous of me, because the moment he started to hate me was one time when he and my mother had been quarrelling all night – I sat in the kitchen, there was just a thin wall to the next room. At one point I got up in the middle of the night, went into the other room, put my arms around my mother and said to him, 'You mustn't talk to my mother like that.' From that moment he hated me for the next five years. He wouldn't let me go out either, and if I did he would stand on the balcony and shout 'Whore!' at me so everyone in the whole neighbourhood could hear. He was absolutely insane. He was one of the old Russian aristocracy brought up never to do a day's work in his life – a tartar of the old aristocracy – he hated the Reds more than anything, he had complete paranoia, he thought that they were under his bed and that every one of my friends was a Russian spy. [*Laughter.*]

* You said before that it was three years before you found the security to paint – how did you find it?
Coming to Bristol. I was travelling around Europe for a year with another girl. She was sixteen and I was seventeen and that was quite unusual then. We hitched all over the place, down Spain and up again – this at the time of the Suez crisis. We managed to get back to Paris and she went to spend Christmas with her family but my grandparents had written a letter to me saying, 'Don't come back, we don't want to see you,' asking my mother to tell me that as well. I was proud and I said, 'I'm not bloody going back, fuck them, I'm staying on my own in Paris.' I was staying in a cold room, no heating, it was quite a thing, December, and I didn't have hardly any clothes and was working in art school to get some money. At this time I met this guy who was from Bristol, and he was a kind person, the same age as me, and lived in a tiny little

room in an attic and gave English lessons. So I moved in and we started some kind of a relationship, not because there was a great love thing, but it just happened to work out like that because I was on my own. I got accidentally pregnant, and for various reasons we got married. Stevan's parents had a little semi-detached house in Bristol where we lived rent free for about a year. There was a little studio I could have – it was a little glass veranda that I made into a studio. He was making jewellery and I was painting.

* Did you paint women right from the start? What kind of things were you into?

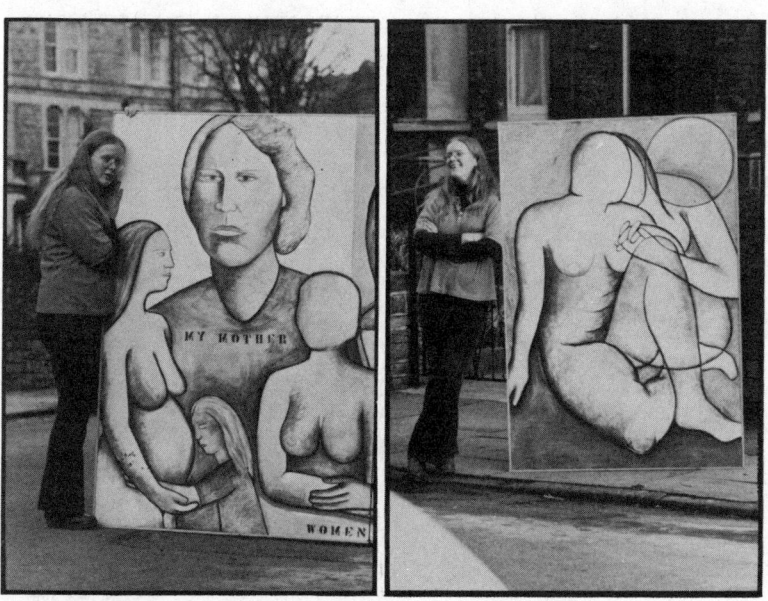

No, no. I spent a year doing lots of drawing, and going unofficially to evening classes at the art school doing sculpture. It was very important for me working three-dimensionally – I very much like clay and I liked doing it. Stevan's mother is somewhat of a feminist in her outlook, very supportive of me – she unquestioningly accepted me for what I was. Then I did some drawings when I was drunk and I did a whole series of drawings of how I saw things when drunk in very clear blacks and whites and much more intense light. They were quite good and the first really inspired work I'd done. I was into working with colour and form because I didn't go to art school and I had to learn the craft before I could actually start expressing what I wanted to express. so it wasn't until a few years later, after Toivo was born naturally at home, fourteen years ago. I know that I had been trying to express a sense of space and light and form of things that didn't conform to any men's conception at all . . . I mean men didn't seem to recognize my sense of space. I didn't understand clearly at the time because I was completely on my own and there were no other women I

could compare notes with, so I was made to feel like a freak. This was ten years before the Women's Movement. I never met any other women at all who questioned anything. The birth of Toivo was an amazing experience . . . I was alone in this room, and he was born before anybody came. It was a spiritual, cosmic experience as well as a physical bloody one – a combination of both. I did a painting – pretty abstract – of this experience – the body of a woman and her bloody womb – there was a piece of wood coming out of the painting so it was very obviously flesh and blood – this child coming out . . . and there were planets and space. I put it into a little exhibition in Bristol, my first one ever.

* And what was the reaction?
All the other work was non-figurative – there was a visitors' book, and some people, including women, had written how disgusting, how obscene and how crude, and how could I do a painting like that? It really surprised me, because I thought I had done a good piece of work, perhaps the best I'd ever done. As a woman, the experience I'm having is supposed not to be the subject-matter for art. It was taboo to do this. I felt very instinctively that there was something bloody wrong about this. The experience changed my whole life, my whole outlook on myself as a woman; I felt so strongly that this was a very genuine real thing, and I wasn't going to betray it. From that point on I worked figuratively, because I was going to explore this sphere. I did a whole lot of work exploring sexual imagery – but it was heterosexual. I read a book by Robert Graves, *The White Goddess*, which changed my outlook, because I never realized that there was a very different religion before, and I hadn't known that there had been a whole other women's culture.

* You've been doing quite a bit of research on that, haven't you?
Yes. Ever since, I've read everything I can find that's got to do with matriarchy and women's culture. Coming from Sweden, where women have gained a certain amount of freedom, sexual and otherwise, living in England in a marriage where we are treated as a man's shadow . . . that was quite a shock to me. Having two small children I felt very oppressed by the situation, and not knowing any other women artists, seeing TV, films, media of all kinds, pornography, advertising, all these images of women always belittling, always denying what women are. The only images I found that conveyed strength of women were from very ancient Greece. I could connect it up with Robert Graves, so I set about the task of finding what it was that was being conveyed to me . . . I was getting such strong vibes from these images, these women, so I started to explore that in my painting . . . re-creating what those women were about, I felt this very strong, mystic thing of being used as a medium for some kind of feminine power. Like the goddess

is rising again – I felt I was an instrument in forwarding this – I still believe that it is so.

* When you realized you were a lesbian, did that bring about a change in your painting?
I realized a lot later, especially after reading Charlotte Wolff's book *Love Between Women*, where she talks of a new theory of Sapphic analysis, the ancient cultures. It really clicked with me about ancient women, the matriarchal societies, and how present-day lesbian women would be most like the ancient woman in character. They were not like the heterosexual women of today whose sexuality is stunted to suit the male. The feeling I got in my own studies was very clear – that the ancient women were bisexual in every way, physically, psychically, in all ways. It struck me much later that was the message I was getting from the images of the ancient women, that that was what I had been looking for without being aware of it. All along, when I'd been showing my paintings, I was accused for years of being a lesbian, long before I knew I was. They were strong images of strong women and men felt threatened by them, saying they were ugly, calling me a lesbian.

* That's how it works. If you are strong, you must be a lesbian because you don't fit into the norm of femininity. It's what's always put on strong women.
Yes. It's a very important part of one's strength to not deny half of one's being. How can anyone be strong who is suppressing half their being?

* When you realized you were a lesbian, your artistic and sexual and sensual sensitivities melded together. You seem to have been moving towards that unity all the time . . .
Yes.

* When did you first realize you were a lesbian?
The first idea of that possibility was when I was about twenty-five and was getting out of my first marriage. I met a group of artists who were bisexual and it was the first time I had come across any people who were open about it. There was a woman in the group who was a poet, and she started to bring me out, and made me feel as if I was beautiful again, because I felt really dowdy being with two small kids all the time and living with this guy, which was a real drag. It was because of that I got some confidence in my own

identity again. I had a very short thing with her, but it frightened me, probably 'cos she was quite a little woman, very beautiful in a very feminine way with a very strong mind. I was put in the situation of feeling like the big butch freak, which at the time I couldn't take, having had that put on me all my life.

* Go on – what happened?
I was perfectly aware at that time about what was happening, but I fell in love with a guy who was very beautiful – long hair, and very feminine, and I lived with him for a year and a half.

* Did you think about what happened with this woman, or did you push it to the back of your mind?
After that I always thought of myself as definitely bisexual. I was always reaching out in that direction, but never being able to take the complete step, and it's only really through the Women's Movement, as with many other women . . . it's the support of other women – not feeling a freak any more, that's the main thing.

* So it was after you became involved with the Women's Movement?
It was seeing lesbian women in the movement and feeling the energy being vibrated by them – just watching lesbian women dancing with each other was a revelation for me. The whole thing I had been looking for in women suddenly was there. Some of my paintings came after that, coming back from a conference where women had been dancing altogether in the nude. I did a series of paintings that released a hidden feeling of joy at last after all those years.

* Were you very attracted to women during this period you called yourself bisexual? Fancying them and just not doing anything about it?
Yes – but I was living in Sweden at this time and it was a much more difficult situation in Sweden.

* Why is it more difficult? What's the gay scene like there?
Even now, the Women's Movement in Sweden has been incredibly straight. It's only in the last year or so that the lesbian front has begun to make a real impact. For years before that the few gay women in the movement had not come to the surface at all and there has been a real put-down of them, and, of course, in Sweden this

whole thing of sexual liberalism – there's not the same heavy oppressiveness.

* Oppressive tolerance?
Exactly. There's heavy pressure on all girls from their teens to screw around with men the whole time. It's the opposite pressure – it's sexually liberal only for the bloke's pleasure – but it's really difficult to see through that. The sexual revolution bit – it's heavy – lesbianism is seen as titillation for commercial gain.

* You were saying that lesbianism is very popular in porn clubs.
That's right – it's the height of radicalism – to have a lesbian cabaret.

* It sounds quite a suffocating environment. How do women in the lesbian front cope with it?
Most of them are very much under cover at the moment – this year at the International Women's Day march I walked with the Victoria group, with banners and posters actually saying what we were, and it's the first time in Sweden's history that a group of lesbians has walked openly down the street. I have worked politically for years in Sweden. I joined all the left-wing groups from Maoists to Anarchists to Trotskyists, to try and find out what they actually thought and were into. I organized Vietnam exhibitions all around Sweden which gave me an opportunity to confront all the artists about their political attitudes, which was quite an eye-opener. All the time I was worried and I would say, 'What are the women doing? What are they doing that relates to women? Why aren't there any other women at the meetings?' And it was always like saying something obscene – not the sort of thing you should mention.

* When I used to say things like that to the men I worked with in the left, they used to say things like, 'We don't oppress women, any woman can come along to any of our meetings, say what they like, make a speech, write a pamphlet or whatever,' but in fact there was no recognition of the basic mechanics of oppression and how even just the presence of men can totally inhibit most women from pushing themselves forward.
When I came into one of these left-wing groups, my experience had been of marriage for eight years, two kids and feeling completely oppressed, my mother dying in poverty, and I said, 'What are you talking about? How does that relate to either mine or my

mother's experience? Nothing, nothing at all.' So I thought there was a huge lie there somewhere. This is why I was never willing after that to work in a mixed group or in the straight left . . . after the Women's Movement – never again. And it's lesbians – who truly have no interest or anything invested anywhere else than with women who can see the clearest – because as long as you relate to men you come behind them. I can't sit here and be smug and say lesbian women are better. One must be honest about this – the majority of women have no choice in the matter, whether they live with men or not – the plain economic poverty of all women – which is why I work with the 'Wages for Housework' movement.

* How do you see the future of the Women's Movement – is it progressing?
I don't know. All I do know is that we are the future, we are the only people with anything of relevance to say. I just have this blind belief that it has to happen, women have to rise, or that's the end of everything – as Robin Morgan says, 'This time we will be free, or no one will survive.'

* It's difficult to see how.
Oh yes.

* Doesn't that depress you?
After going through ten years of isolation, I can't ever feel as depressed as that again. I always have hope and optimism because to me it's fantastic that there is a movement at all.

* You must get joy and strength from your paintings, paintings for women?
Yes, yes.

* I get a lot of joy and strength from your paintings, I must say; sitting here just now I was thinking it's like having people in the room. What reaction have you had from the art establishment to your work?
Well there was that famous occasion when Beverley Skinner and I had an exhibition at the art college here in Bristol four years ago, and I have never met so much hostility in my whole life, and that's saying something. There were all these beautiful-looking, trendy, long-haired young men and women. Apparently the whole art college saw the exhibition and they were all discussing it and they all hated it. On the first day they put a notice on the wall stating that

this exhibition has absolutely nothing to do with women's ambitions or feelings about themselves.

* That's not the only time that's happened to you, is it? What is it in your paintings that people find so disturbing?

It wasn't only the content of the work, it was also the fact that it was figurative, it's against the whole trend in English art, which is complete mystification, very trendy and gimmicky. Figurative work is seen as bad in itself, and what I was saying was even worse. For example, the fact that I use letters and words in my paintings is seen as against all the aesthetic rules. One of my paintings puts

together some images from advertising, like faceless women showing their hairdos and a porn image of a woman, just standing in the nude; combined with, in the front, two Chinese women looking right out of the picture with guns on their shoulders – no smile or anything – just completely sort of, 'Here I am' . . . not pleasing anybody – and that painting – all the men who came up to my place, whatever they were like, reacted in an incredibly aggressive manner to the painting and made comments like,

'Obviously you think you are a sex object, do you?' because I had written on it, 'Sex, sex, I'm a sex object' on these faceless women, and on the other side there was this crying woman and underneath it said, 'The reality – neurosis and misery.' You can compare bourgeois male paintings since the Renaissance with modern advertising pornography and the way women are shown and seen by men (even in what's called 'fine art' in painting), is nothing but porn, placing women's bodies smiling like it's all to do with the male spectator and the male buyer – and that's, what men are used to seeing, even in painting.

* Well, I think there's something – looking at your paintings – that men are shut out from, isn't there? They can't respond to them like we can because the message is very heavy to them – to us it means a lot . . .
Yes, well, I was looking at other women as strong, beautiful human beings with dignity –

* Well, that is a threat, isn't it?
Oh yes, a complete threat in our culture – like when my painting 'God giving birth' was almost banned for blasphemy and obscenity at Swiss Cottage – in a way I would have liked them to have taken me to court because I would have liked to stand up in court and first of all ask whether the image of a woman giving birth to a child is an obscenity, and secondly, what do they think about all these degrading images of women they see all around them – to me that is an obscenity. Some women artists have been into showing the suffering female – that's one way of going about it – to show your pain – and you see I just could not do that because that's exactly what the guys like – they like you to sort of lay yourself open – show your pain and suffering – that's perfectly OK, but what they can't stand is women who are strong.

* Yes, that's one thing I've always felt about the Women's Movement, and about the whole thing of being a lesbian – there's lots of freak-outs, but you've got to put forward the strength and you've got to give other women confidence.

* Kate Millett says that in *Flying*, doesn't she? What she said about one of the meetings when the Radical Lesbians walked in – how it gave her such a big charge – and that's the thing about lesbian women – how they've got that real strength.

Obviously all along I have had a kind of woman-identified way of looking at women because for many years I was reacting incredibly strongly in relation to getting really upset about women being put down. I've been in situations – years back – when we were at a party or something, and some woman was upset and turning to me for support and some bloody guy dragging me away – this kind of thing – and it always upset me tremendously. I felt more oppressed as a married heterosexual woman with children than I have as a lesbian – I know that I feel better now – I would find it difficult to say which time in my life I felt the most oppressed. It's something I feel has become increasingly clear from things like the battered wives' houses and the rape thing . . . what is happening to all women . . . there are so many women all over the world who are out of duty having to screw their men and being raped if they refuse, and getting nothing out of it whatsoever. There isn't any work outside that situation – you can't make a living for yourself in any way whatsoever – what choice do we have in countries like Italy, for instance?

* Yes – what about the liberated men of Portugal beating up the women in the abortion march?
Yes – like I said – at the International Conference on Wages for Housework, in London when we presented the whole thing on lesbian women to the rest of them – there was a group of Italian women there – they'd never even thought of it – they completely came out in solidarity – they said they could totally understand what we were saying. They came from Italy, and it's just like another world, one mustn't forget that . . .

* I see the Church as one of the worst enemies of women . . .
Yes . . . oh yes. The Church . . . I hate it . . . the Roman Catholic Church . . .

* The Church of England as well – it's probably not as oppressive . . .
The Catholic Church of Italy . . .

* Islam and Hinduism as well . . .
Islam is the ultimate . . . I mean it's Islamic peoples who are performing clitorectomies on young girls, and that's spreading apparently, not lessening, today – I've got this book by a couple of Swedish women, it's geographical and historical about women all

around the world. They give a description of clitorectomy and say how it's still spreading.It's a very deliberate attempt at mutilating women . . . I mean we in the West are being sort of psychologically mutilated, and they're being actually physically mutilated.

* A lot of women don't seem to realize that a lot of men are actually working at a counter-offensive against the Women's Movement . . .
In what ways do you mean?

* I think that rape ruling was a counter-attack.
Yes.

* (A) I think that the Sex Discrimination Bill is a counter-attack – I think it was a very clever piece of propaganda – and the Abortion Amendment Bill.

* (J) Do you want to ask Monica about her exhibition?

* (A) Yes, how long ago was that?
It was this year – in January [1975].

* What was it exactly?
A Swedish woman artist, famous artist, happened to see our exhibition at Swiss Cottage two years ago and she was offered an exhibition in the south of Sweden and she asked the gallery to invite me to exhibit with her, and that was the beginning two years back – we called our joint exhibition 'Women's Lives', and then that travelled round to Norway and different places in Sweden, and then in January there was a coming together of our exhibition – parts of it – with about seven other groups of women to do this very huge women's collective exhibition – it was a vast exhibition in something called the 'House of Culture' in the centre of Stockholm – the cultural committee in Stockholm actually put about 20,000 quid into it, and it covered just about every aspect of women's history, women's oppression, women's art, textiles, women's ancient culture – the woman artist in history – just about every aspect apart from lesbian women. The only thing in the exhibition that hinted at it was two of my paintings; one called, 'Just trying to find the real me', and another one, 'When are we going to feel joy again?' There was this whole wall and these two were on top, and that was the only thing in the whole exhibition; and also, just to make it more clear, I put up the leaflets advertising the Victoria group on my wall, and I found that when there were write-ups and criticisms about the exhibition it was generally very hostile towards

the whole thing but it was always me that they would say something about like, 'I can't understand Monica Sjöö's view about women,' and I was seen as a sort of ultra-feminist, and in Sweden that is a dirty word – even in the Women's Movement it has been until now – and it was very clear to me that the reason I was singled out was because my work was very much more women-identified, much more clearly so, more politically so, than the other women's work.

* The exhibition was a great success though, wasn't it?

Oh marvellous, fantastic, 60,000 people went to it, mainly women, and all kinds of women, from old-age pensioners to schoolkids, and I was employed by the House of Culture to publicly guide every day for an hour about fifty people at a time, which was like handing it to me on a plate, because it gave me the opportunity to talk to hundreds and hundreds of people personally, and all the knowledge I'd gathered from working in the movement for five years – just about every campaign from the Abortion Campaign to the Claimants' Union – I really had quite a lot of experience from working in the movement; and the whole history of matriarchal culture and everything – I could discuss it all with them, and what's more, I got paid to do it – £16 for an hour's work! I was the only one who was free during the day to do it, as I was travelling . . . the others had commitments like kids, and so on . . . it was advertised in the press: Monica Sjöö is the guide . . . it was very good that they asked me to do it . . .

Pat Arrowsmith

*Pat Arrowsmith is forty-five. She went to
Cheltenham Ladies College (from which she was
suspended) and later read history at Cambridge,
psychology at Ohio University and social science at
Liverpool University. She is well known for her
activities as a pacifist, for which she has been sent
to prison nine times. The first time was in 1958, the
most recent 1974. She has been on hunger strike in
prison for political reasons and has been forcibly
fed. During her last sentence she escaped and was
put in solitary confinement for helping to try and
form a prisoners' union. Pat is a writer and
painter in her spare time. Five of her books have
been published and her paintings and drawings
have been in a number of exhibitions in London. At
present she works in the Secretariat of Amnesty
International.*

* Pat, you're probably most well known for activities with CND
and the Troops Out Movement, and being involved in radical
political activities for quite a long time. In the last few years we've
seen the rise of the Women's Movement, and we haven't really seen
your name attached to this very much. We wondered why you are
particularly active in these other fields and why you haven't got
into the Women's Movement?

True, I suppose. I think that I have the feeling that people disperse
themselves into too many activities and really I've felt a bit guilty
not being more active in the Women's Movement. It's not quite
true, I've been on a number of marches, and I was involved with
GLF very slightly at the beginning. I suppose that's really the
reason, I'm first and foremost a pacifist, someone who believes in
social change by non-violent resistance, not violent direct action.
I've been involved primarily in the anti-war movement, starting
with the nuclear disarmament movement. I suppose the thing that
struck me as the most horrifying possibility was the human race

destroying itself, nothing else at any time has seemed so dreadful. I've been involved in race relations in the United States years ago and a little in this country. I think I've seen myself as having something of a useful role as a lesbian – well for about a year or two now – if I've been in a situation where it was relevant for somebody to get up speaking as a homosexual, I've always done this at meetings and so on. In more recent times, if I've been interviewed by a newspaper, as I was by the *Observer* for their International Women's Year thing, I decided to state quite firmly that I was a homosexual, and you know I think this in itself is a fairly useful contribution.

* When were you first aware that you were a lesbian?
I went to a girls' boarding school and I was aware of being homosexual. I was very much in love with another woman, another girl, I mean. It never came to anything, I was very worried, you know. I hoped 'this is a phase that I will get out of'. I remember at Cheltenham, one of my schools, we had these sex talks telling you all about the facts of life, so they got out all these nice slides with all kinds of cocks and things on them. It was all quite interesting and we were invited at the end to ask any question we wanted confidentially, of the person who was lecturing. We could be assured of a good hearing, we weren't to be afraid to ask anything, and I was very involved with my best friend. We weren't having an affair or anything, she sensed this and wasn't too happy about it, and I felt very guilty about this. It seemed to me quite unacceptable. Anyway, I was about seventeen or eighteen and I should have been getting interested in boys by then and this was a contemporary of mine, we were both in the same class.

* It's acceptable when you're thirteen?
More or less, provided it's called a passion, but this was getting on, I should have been dating boys. Being at boarding school I never met any. Anyway, at the end of the lecture I asked about this and was told that I must eschew this unhealthy friendship.

* Did you know for certain that you were a lesbian then, or did you just . . .?
What do you mean by that? Depends on your definition of terms. I knew that I wanted to have a sexual relationship with this friend of mine, I knew the word 'lesbian' and I accepted that I had a lesbian feeling, and I had no doubt that I wanted sex with various girls

from the age of twelve on, and I knew what it was I wanted. I didn't accept that I was a lesbian for ever and a day, indeed I wasn't, because I had very close involvements with one or two men.

* Did you ever – you weren't married at all, were you?
No, no, no. Well, I consider myself married now to the woman I live with, but not married in the heterosexual sense, no. When I left school I hoped it would all go, you know, that it would all go away, and that I'd get interested in boys. Surprisingly, in a way it did. I don't think I was ever uninterested in women at any time, but when I went to Cambridge, I fell very much in love with a bloke who I was involved in politics with there. We were both in the World Government Movement. I was absolutely crazy about him and he wasn't interested in me. We were quite close friends, but then I had the nearest thing I'd ever had to an affair with a man. I was very much in love with him and we thought about getting married. Then he left Cambridge before I did and went to Canada, and that was the end of him. And the only other man I've had, apart from boy-friends I went out with who didn't mean anything to me, was an American. It was half, half a kind of sibling relationship and half an erotic one. I met him not very long ago, years and years later, it was interesting that he had become a homosexual himself.

* Have you had many relationships with women?
Not very many. Well, I've only ever . . . well, I've only had two, I suppose – well, I only lived with one woman in the way I've lived with Wendy. I've had three other close relationships with women, a very unsatisfactory one in the sense that the woman resisted very much in her own mind and resisted me. We lived in the same town and it was the first actual – how shall I put it? – consummated lesbian relationship I'd ever had. That was someone I met in a hostel in Chester and I was in my middle twenties, a year or two older than her. We had a sort of on-off relationship for about a year, we didn't live together, and I was heartbroken at the end of it. Then I went away, left Chester and came to London and became involved with the Peace Movement. And then there was somebody I worked with in the movement who I was very much in love with for years, but she was straight, she wasn't interested in me. She was as straight as

anybody ever is, I think, so that was rather an unhappy time, and then I met Wendy. Aside from that, there have been one or two people.

* And how long have you been together?
Fourteen years.

* Fourteen years, that's a long time . . .
Like any marriage, it's had its vicissitudes.

* In what sense do you see it as a marriage?
Well, I'd always seen it as something that would continue. We put our lives together in the way that people do when they marry, we

never got down and swore fidelity to each other – that doesn't mean anything anyway. We regard our possessions in common, we do things together, we share a place, we both, I think, viewed this as something that would go on. That's all a marriage really does mean. Maybe it won't. But, I mean that anything can happen, as in any marriage.

* It's a surprising term to use, isn't it, in a modern-day context. Can you talk generally about relationships between anyone,

whether they're male/female, female and female or male and male? Do you see it as important that people are faithful to each other, sexually faithful?

I can only answer with a truism. I mean it's only important if it's important to them. I don't know really. I mean, in my marriage, I've not stayed wholly faithful to Wendy or she to me – I think that one of the problems that can arise is that if you think one person is going to get hurt – or if you don't want it to end – or if you're afraid of jealousy, and you conceal what's going on – it removes an element of trust from your relationship inevitably – because you fall into the trap of dishonesty. This can be one of the great losses and I don't know how you work round it. I really don't know any neat answers to these types of things at all, I don't think there are any.

* Why is it important for you to see your relationship as a marriage?
Well, I tell you, I'm a very insecure person – you ask me why I'm into marriage. Well, a lot of my life is very volatile, I've been in and out of prison a lot, I haven't got an ordinary career, I'm in my middle forties, I've looked for anchorage in personal relationships which I may not find in a sort of group thing. I want to feel that there's this person that I've got a long-term involvement with, and the longer you're with a person, the more interwoven you become in a way. You may have your rows and stuff and you have the common shared experiences, jokes and fun things, and you don't want to lose it really, that seems to point to the future. Sometimes there is a problem, you want to do all this, but at the same time you very likely do fall in love with somebody else. How do you reconcile these two totally contradictory things? Because they are quite contradictory really, that's the difficulty.

* How long have you been out of the closet?
I don't really know. I don't remember a time particularly when I announced that I was a homosexual. Just gradually more and more I've not bothered to conceal the fact. It's been easy for me, you see, because working in left-wing politics and the Peace Movement, the sort of people I've met – anyone could be intolerant, I know – but, out of all the possible milieus there might have been, then it would have been the most tolerant and relaxed probably. I can't remember the first time I said to somebody, 'I'm homosexual.' I just take it

for granted that people know I'm a lesbian. I mean I only have one problem which most homosexuals have, and that's my parents, and that's mainly because they are so very old and they're invalids and very religious and my father's a clergyman.

* You've never been aware of any feelings against you in the left-wing movement because of your homosexuality?
Not very consciously. You sense that the men are rather resentful, and whether it's just because you're a woman or apparently a forthright woman, or maybe because you're a lesbian, it's hard to tell, but most of the men who I've had to do with in recent years wouldn't care to admit it anyway. I suppose in a sense I came out in my novel to some extent. I wrote a novel about women in prison which could only have been written by a lesbian, I think, even though it wasn't an autobiographical novel – I mean, it was auto-biography in a way. In prison it might be said you come out because it's the norm in a women's prison. It's a sought-after thing to be a lesbian anyway, so there's no great bother about coming out of any closet in prison. And I think that helped me quite a bit actually, to be in an environment where it's quite normal and desirable to be gay, to be queer as it was then called.

* When was it that you first went into Holloway?
The first time I was in Holloway was in 1958.

* And was it very openly gay, the same thing then as it is now?
Yes, but I was only in for a very short sentence – about two weeks. But, yes, there were a lot of fairly obvious gay women around.

* Do you think it's more . . . we've heard lots of stories about Holloway from other women, and it seems to be packed with dykes these days.
A lot of women are looking for a mock cock while they're in there. They may be basically straight women, or maybe they haven't discovered that side of themselves. There's a lot of role-playing, probably a bit less last time I was in than the time before, but there was a lot of women really pretending to be men.

* Were they lesbians on the outside, the butch ones?
Some were, but some were on to a good thing. I mean, I remember one woman who came in who was on the game outside. She came in really femme looking and decided to turn inside because of the fags, you know – I mean the perks. She then becomes a lesbian. It's not

a chivalrous thing to be a butch lesbian in Holloway, it's a way of getting your ironing done for you and getting kept in fags. It's quite a mercenary business if you want to handle it that way. Even I could be fooled sometimes with busts strapped back and sanitary towels made to look like a cock.

* Can you wear jeans and trousers?
Oh yes, you can. You can wear your own clothes now, but it used to be funny in the old days when you couldn't and the butches had to do the best they could with shirts rolled up to the elbows and tattoos all down the arms and sideboards back in teddy-boy days, in these cotton frocks. But you'd try very hard to get a job in the gardens or somewhere, where you could wear dungarees. Then you'd see if you could swing it and wear them in the evenings as well, but that wouldn't always work, they wouldn't always let you.

* Did you have any affairs when you were in there?
Yes, about two or three times. Once it was with somebody in on a political charge, the other times were in other prisons anyway.

* What kind of women are in Holloway?
Every kind. At one time I suppose the majority of women would be – now, it's dicey using class terms – but in a certain sense of the word it was mainly working-class women. Not any longer, now there are a lot of highly educated women from colleges in Australia, United States, Jamaica, who are in for smuggling hash and stuff.

* I know you don't have much spare time because you are always going to meetings and so on, but when you do have spare time, how do you tend to fill it?
Well, I like painting, I've always liked painting, it runs in my family. Also I write poetry and I've written one or two books, a couple of novels. I wouldn't pretend that all my spare time is taken up with things like that, I go to the pictures and parties sometimes.

* Do you go to clubs and discos?
Yes, I got to discos and things now and again, and I've been to the Gateways a few times. I don't belong to it, partly because it's too far away from where I live. Been to the Crown and Woolpack quite a few times in the past, been to the odd *Sappho* disco, parties, you know, when people ask us.

* Are most of your friends gay or straight?

Don't know, probably most are straight really. I mean, most of the people I know at all well are people from the political movement I'm in.

* What political movements are you most heavily involved in now?
Oh, Troops Out Movement and British Withdrawal from Northern Ireland Campaign . . . and I like ordinary things like going for country walks, play tennis rather badly, swim at Hampstead Ponds. It's got gayer and gayer over the years.

* You've been going there a long time?
Oh yeah, Wendy and I discovered it about ten years ago, I suppose, and we've been going every summer since and it's got gayer and gayer year by year. At first there was one identifiable group of gay women, we never got talking to them or they to us, but I mean suddenly last summer . . . [Laughter.]

* What do you think about role-playing?
I think anyone does what they like. Different things at different times. I think it's all nonsense, you know.

* I think I'd find that quite heavy in Holloway, the butch-femme role-playing.
Wendy and I are not particularly femme-like looking women and I remember coming out of Holloway after one sentence and feeling, Oh dear, it's all wrong, you know, I'd got this butch/femme so much into me through being in there I felt a bit of a sort of queer queer, and rather uneasy about it. In fact this theme looms in my novel with one of the characters, so in that way maybe there is some autobiography in it. It came as a relief really, when the gay movement got going here, to find that it was all rubbish and sort of wasn't with us any more. I think rigid role-playing is a bit silly – I said that anyone should do their own thing – of course they should, but if women are going to ape all the worst characteristics in men and simply become male chauvinistic pigs themselves in their butchness, then that's wrong. If one isn't going to accept it in a man then one surely isn't going to accept it in a woman. And, as you know, I think women ought to do better than men when it comes to pacifism and violence. If men have used the gun to do well, then women should find another way of doing it.

* Well, there are women like Golda Meir and Indira Ghandi who aren't going too well.

Well, there is *Ms* Thatcher as well.

* (A) Raving lunatic.

* (J) Well, there's always in a thing like that a certain number of renegades aren't there?

* (A) Have you ever felt . . . have you ever wanted a child?

No, not really, I've never wanted consciously to have children. I'm not someone who particularly likes other people's children on the spot, the opposite really, I think they're a nuisance. On the other hand I worked in a children's home, and in the context of them being there all the time, you got quite fond of some of them, but I'm not someone who instantly turns on to children, like I instantly turned on to your tabby cat for instance. They're a bit of a nuisance really, and I think a lot of women, if they were honest, would say the same thing. They fuck up a conversation and get in the way at a social evening. They break things, they pee all over the place. They are like great lumps of sour anthropomorphic ice-cream.

* What do you think are the most important things that have come out of your relationship with Wendy?

Oh God, I don't know, I don't find that at all easy to answer. The mutual caring, the mutual concern for each other, the things you've shared together, the jokes. In our case it all started on a very basic level. I mean we met through the Peace Movement, something that was of great importance to us, of great significance. We didn't just meet socially, and this had a pretty binding effect, and we've worked together as colleagues in the same office over a period of time, so it was a very meaningful relationship.

* It must have been very difficult for you both when you were in prison.

Well, I think it was probably worse for Wendy in a way. She was outside and she was in the situation of, well, hopefully, missing me, whereas I was in a different world, like being in another country really. I don't know that you miss anything exactly, you just have to adjust . . . I'm not bad at adjusting to new and bizarre situations. I sort of adapt to prison, it's probably easier when you are a lesbian. One thing in prison is that you're not lonely actually, whereas, I suppose, she must have quite often felt lonely outside with myself not there.

* What do you get out of your poetry and paintings?
Money, I hope. [*Laughter*.]

* Is that the most important thing?
Oh no, ego trips, I don't know. I suppose it's – the sense of having created something, but certainly I wouldn't get anything out of any of these things if – certainly out of writing – if they weren't published or read because it's a sheer waste of time. Writing, to my mind, is another sort of talking, so if nobody reads it, it's like talking to an empty room.

* Do you see your paintings as communication?
Not in quite the same way. I mean, it is a real pleasure actually doing them, whereas writing a book can be quite laborious, only some of it's an actual pleasure. I think I could enjoy being on a desert island with some pictures. I like some of my own pictures, I quite like looking at them, nobody else has to, but I don't especially want to sit reading and re-reading one of my own poems, if you can make that sort of comparison. People sometimes say the important thing is to have written it, I say, oh balls, it's a sheer waste of time unless somebody reads it. It's totally frustrating and I've written six novels, and I've only had two of them published so I know what I'm talking about. I wrote my first novel when I was fifteen and it hasn't been published yet; the second I wrote when I was eighteen. So I knew all about writing novels, and not having them published, and what a bore it is, and living in a basement on cracked eggs while you're doing it. I was a cinema usherette for two years while I was writing one of them.

* Is there anything specific you'd love to say?
Let there be peace – with justice and socialism.

Luchia Fitzgerald

Luchia Fitzgerald is twenty-eight. She was born in Cork in a mother and baby home for illegitimate children. She was brought up by her grandmother and went to a convent school in Tramore. She left school at twelve to work child-minding and washing-up. She ran away from home at fifteen to her mother in Rochdale and worked in a cotton-mill. After nine months she ran away again to Manchester where she worked in a café. She was picked up by the police and eventually put in the Bolton Hostel for Runaway Minors until she was nineteen. Next she returned to Manchester where she worked on the buses for a year. She joined GLF in 1971 and became involved in the Women's Movement in 1972. In 1974 she started the Northern Women's Liberation Rock Band with six other women. From 1972 to 1975 she lived and worked in the Manchester Women's Centre and started a Battered Wives' House in 1974. At present she lives in Manchester and runs an offset litho press with other women.

* You left school at twelve and then you went to work. What was it like? Did you have many friends who did that?
Oh, yeah, I mean it was the done thing, you weren't any different from anybody else – to leave school and go out and graft. Working-class kids had to do it anyway.

* As an illegitimate child were you treated any differently?
I wasn't treated any differently by anybody else except my family . . . they were the only ones . . . in fact I got a lot of support from neighbours and people outside because they knew what was going on in the family as far as I was concerned, but there was nothing they could do about it. I used to get beat something

shocking, you know, whereas in this country you can be had up for it . . . They were all at it – if either of the lads had a row with their wife they'd come home and take it out on me. My uncles they were.

* At the bottom of the ladder, weren't you – a woman, a working-class woman, illegitimate, not much education, in a country like Ireland?
Yeah, well it's terrible – women are oppressed in every way there. They don't go out like, like women do over here. It's changed a bit now, but in them days it was terribly oppressive. All the men went out together to the pub at night, the women would sit home in their own houses, and if they went visiting each other they were called gossipers, so they didn't do it. They were totally separated from each other.

* Kept isolated from each other?
All the time, yeah, and like I say, if they were seen out together during the day they were just called gossipers, and nobody ever wanted the name of a gossiper.

* And what about the Church – what did it mean being a Catholic when you were young?
It made me feel guilty about everything, especially about the gay thing because I read once in this religious book that God, like, burnt this whole village of homosexuals when he was working, when he was doing his rounds like. That made me feel really awful, you know, I literally almost went to give myself up.

* Did you realize you were a lesbian when you were really young?
I must have been eight or nine.

* What made you realize it?
I had no eyes for men and stuff like that. I didn't know what I was, but I knew I was different.

* And did you believe in God, the Church, priests at the time?
Well, I did at the time, I mean that's why I felt so badly, as I said, went to give myself up rather than them come in a year's time to pick me up. I thought I won't fucking give in to that, I'll go and say, 'Take me and lock me up now,' because I knew that they locked anyone up who wasn't, you know, straight run-of-the-mill.

* How old were you then, Luchia?

About twelve.

* And you actually knew then that the homosexuals in the book you read, that that was you?
Yeah, yeah. But I couldn't identify meself with the filth that I read in that book. I mean I looked at meself as filth, and I knew in years to come that I couldn't keep it down all the time, or hide it all the time, so that's why I thought I'd give meself up.

* And did you?
Did I, fuck! [*Laughter.*]

* When did you give up your belief in religion?
When I was eighteen. After I had come to England and after about a year in the gay scene and talked to different people about religion. I just completely fucked it all up – I mean it took me up until about two years ago to just be able to say Our Lady was no fucking virgin, I can *say* that now and I don't give a fuck, but one time I couldn't say that. It took me a long time to actually throw it off completely. I mean, you still feel a bit guilt-ridden about different things, you know.

* When was your first lesbian affair? How old were you?
When I was twelve. I was just ready for leaving school and I got a job on the fair, you know, like it's the local fair, it's there all the time. I started fancying one of the women off the fair and I told her. We had necking sessions and cuddling sessions and stuff like that. I was in love with this girl from when I was ten, right up until I was about fifteen. I still couldn't get her out of my mind.

* And how did she feel about it?
Oh, she just laughed – she was very affectionate toward me, we were the best of friends, but she was in no way gay, she was too much into men even at ten, know what I mean? She was as much into men as I was into women, but we didn't let that come between us as I thought it was just nice anyway to be friends with someone you like that way. There was no sex at that time, just the kissing – it was just so important to be with her because I loved her so much.

* Was that your last affair, the one at the fairground, before you came to England?
Oh no. I was in love with quite a few people at home, you know what I mean, but I had to keep it down like. And then when I

came to England I started falling in love with women. I say love, because it felt like I was in love, but of course it wasn't. There were women in the factory where I worked and stuff like that. Then I heard about these funny pubs down Manchester, so I started coming down there. It took me a lot of courage to come down there because I was actually facing myself, you know.

* You were frightened then . . .
Of course I was, I was shit scared. I was afraid in case I wasn't all I was thinking I was.

* And what was it like, the place you went to in Manchester?
It was the straight gay scene, which totally knocked me off my feet. Shocked I was that some women were dressed as men. I couldn't understand that because I fucking hated them, and I couldn't understand how women like you or like me, that had the same feelings as me towards other women, were dressed up like men. I wasn't accepted at first on the gay scene because I was fancying women dressed up as men and I was fancying feminine women as well, so people used to call me an in-betweener. But after about six months of that I couldn't stand it any more, so I thought, I look ridiculous in a fucking skirt so I went and had the crop like.

* Short back and sides?
Yeah, and into the suit.

* You chose the butch role – why?
Because I wasn't feminine. I didn't feel feminine in me head – I mean, I used to think like a man towards women. I was pushed into it. If I had been left on me own I would have been all right, but I was pushed into this role.

* Because the whole scene was like that?
Yes, I had to be one or the other. Now I was never a very feminine person – right – I didn't like what the feminine thing portrayed and I was always used to fucking rough work anyway and I just wasn't feminine. I had to choose that role and the simple reason was I would have looked ridiculous dressed up as a femme. I would have felt a freak if I had got meself all tarted up, so I didn't do it, I went the opposite way. That freaked me out too, don't get me wrong.

* (A) It's really understandable.

* (J) When I was first on the gay scene, I chose to be butch, not femme.

* (A) Me too, in my leather jacket.

* (J) Did you go to the pubs and clubs in Manchester? What were they like?
They were all mixed – when I says mixed I mean gays, hetero-sexuals, the fucking lot. There was always a man around every corner waiting to screw you, thinking that's going to put you right, like, you know.

* (J) Yeah, same old trip.

* (A) How long were you involved in that scene, Luchia?
For about five or six years.

* What got you out of it?
I started drinking a lot because I was getting really fucking mixed up. I didn't feel that this was what I wanted out of life. I wanted to be gay but in a different way. I didn't want to . . . I couldn't put words on it, but the word I know is 'oppressed'. I didn't want to oppress anyone and I didn't want to oppress meself. I felt as if I was making a fool of meself in the end, and there was no way out of it – this was all there was for me. So I started drinking and taking drugs, the fucking lot, you know. And I was getting to be a right wreck. Due to the fact that I'd gone like that I couldn't get work the way I looked. I couldn't go back, I just couldn't move, I was stuck . . . in a box. So I was pissed drunk one night down the gay club and I could hear this conversation goin' on the back of me with this woman about how you don't have to be like this. So I turned around and I cocked me ear up and, to cut a long story short, that was Angela Cooper, you know, the lead singer in our band, and Sue Lindsay. Her and Sue Lindsay are having this conversation at the back about being gay but being yourself. So I got really interested in the conversation – it was a little life-saver for me. I never thought there were meetings of gay people, you know, like just come out and just be what you are and fuck the roles. They were talking about role-playing, you see.

* Was that the early days of GLF?
Yes. So I cottoned on to GLF and joined it. At the time GLF

was men and women. I learned a bit about gay politics, and then there was a big split from the men, and then I went off from GLF into the Women's Movement which . . . I changed again then and here I am. Otherwise I would have wound up like a lot of my friends did in the fucking grave, you know – a lot of them killed themselves . . . at that period, yeah.

* Not knowing how to get out of . . .
Yeah – being so fucked up by playing roles and not just being able to be yourself.

* Did you talk with them about it when you found out?
Yeah, I did. When I joined GLF I insisted those fucking meetings were in the gay pubs, and they were. We had nothing to offer them basically, only the meeting, and it wasn't enough. We started having socials, and then we all got lazy about it and they just died out. Most of the people I knew then that I wanted to take with me out of it left GLF because there was nothing, but I had Angie.

* You'd made friends?
I'd made friends with Angela, you see, and they all looked on Angela and her type like as hippies and stuff, middle classy and they were straight gays, you see.

* So most of the women in the straight gay scene are working-class women?
They are.

* And the Women's Movement is largely middle class.
They would only go so far, do you know what I mean, unless they had a relationship with someone on the other side. Although I wasn't having a relationship with Angela Cooper at the time, but I'd sort of . . . I knew I wasn't going to let go of that.

* Did you have any long-lasting relationships during that five years on the straight gay scene?
Not at all, no. It was one after another. Living with someone you know, shacking up for a short time, then breaking up. I don't know, I must have related with twenty or thirty women, and I don't know how many scenes I've had, they're uncountable, you know. When you get a bit older you think, I can't go on like this.

* So when was your first major relationship?

126

It was with Angela Cooper. Me and Angela was bumming about for ages and then we decided – well, we didn't decide, it just happened that way. We sort of cottoned on to the Women's Movement – they were just starting up the Women's Centre in Manchester and I started going to the meetings. I was very fucked off with the meetings because they were talking about working-class people and I sat and took it for a long time, and then I just burst out at one of the meetings, saying 'I've been coming to meetings here for fucking weeks, and I still don't know what you're fucking talking about.' They start at where

they're at, they didn't ask any questions about where anybody else was at in the room, and I went berserk over that. So, to cut a long story short, anyway, I stayed in it because I saw quite a few of them that was gay there and was quite all right like, you know. So they were looking for someone there to live at the Women's Centre and of course no one would live in it because it was a fucking mess and most of the women up there are pretty middle class and not used to living in shit and didn't realize – you know, if you got a paint brush and what have you in your hand that you could make anything you wanted to.

I said fuck it, I might as well go and live in it, no one else will, someone's got to live in it, it's a worthwhile thing, you see. So I went and lived there and we lived there until last Christmas, four years.

* Didn't you start up a refuge for battered wives?
Yeah, meself and Angela started it off. We squatted this house in Charlton because we were getting a lot of calls from battered women. My mother, she was a battered wife, and I came to the realization then at the Women's Centre about her, and the life she had. And the way she was being battered, and that really struck a fucking chord in me. My mother had visited me several times at the Women's Centre and I told her straight then that I was gay and if she couldn't accept that she'd have to fuck off because I wasn't going to lie for anyone. I don't tell my aunt because she's freaked anyway, and then, you see, that would freak her out worse. But, to cut a long story short, anyway, the old lady come to our place and, fucking Jesus, she said she'd been battered again and that . . . fucking done it. So I went and squatted this house to get a refuge for battered wives. In the meantime my mother got her strength up and left the fucking bloke. She didn't leave him, she kicked him out and she's quite happy now and the refuge is all right you know. We've just got a grant. But I had to retire from it because that nearly drove me cuckoo. I couldn't stand it any more, it was too much pressure being put on me on account of being working class. They used to just shove the women on me and I couldn't take it any more, you know what I mean . . . Go and see Luchia, you know, she'll understand, instead of them trying to understand, do you know what I mean?

* What do you feel about the Women's Movement and the lesbian movement being so composed of middle-class women?
Well, there's fuck-all you can do about it, let's put it that way. You have feelings about it, you think it's a bad thing, but you know that the Women's Movement is middle class, but what can you do? I mean, it's like all organizations, you know what I mean, in this day and age, I mean I think the intellectuals always start the thing off and I want . . . I'm fucking living for the day when I

see the whole thing turned arse upwards. Do you know what I mean?

* Yeah, of course middle-class women have the time, don't they, for a start? And the knowledge. They're not locked up in their homes or in the factory.

Yeah – I mean, the peasants didn't revolt in China fucking out of the blue. It was the middle-class people that led them.

* I was going to ask you, I don't know if you mind me asking this, if you noticed any difference in your sex life between when you were in the butch and femme scene to when you became 'liberated'?

Definitely, definitely, I've changed tremendously. I used to have a lot of hang-ups about sex, and they were because I was brought up in a very repressed . . . like I said, everything was repressed and also that was repressed. And you've a lot of hang-ups about religion, your mother, your family, and all that shit about being illegitimate. I mean you bring that through the years with you. So when I joined the Women's Movement, unconsciously everything was getting sorted out, and I always used to run around feeling sorry for myself. But I found out through the Women's Movement too that there was a fuck of a lot of women – a lot of lesbians and some Irish lesbians that I know as well – that have gone through the same thing, and I've heard of people that have had it a lot worse than me. It didn't make things all right at the time, but then, you know, when I came out to that realization, then the realization of being gay, the religious thing, the sexual thing, all that, all sorted itself out nicely – do you know what I mean?

* Yes, I think we've all gone through that actually, being uptight about your body, being shy.

The first time I ever stripped naked in front of a whole lot of women was when I went to Femø.

* When was that?

About three years ago.

* That's that big women's camp in Denmark, isn't it? On an island?

Yeah. And I went there, like, and when I got off the boat like, and I couldn't believe all these women walking around in their skin.

You know, I kind of pulled me head down a bit. I was there for about three or four hours, and I thought, Fuck, and I ran into the tent and I ripped off all my clothes and I just ran like fuck through the lot. [*Laughter*.] I must have been really red, you know. Like, I've got to shake it off, you know. They're all walking around naked, not ashamed of their bodies. They're not looking at each other in a sexual – see, the sexual thing comes into it as well. People are not looking at each other in a sexual way, and I felt it would be lovely for people to just be like that, and if I could be like that, you know, although of course everybody was, you know. It was smashing, after a couple of hours I didn't give a shit. I felt as though a fucking big weight had been lifted off my shoulders, you know. I mean, I'll tell you something now. I literally had a hump through oppression. When Angela Cooper met me, she'll tell you this – I was walking, you know – I had a fucking hump.

* What, a humped back?
Yeah, I was gone right down like that, if you know what I mean, and the longer I was in the Women's Movement, the more it seemed to straighten itself up. That's the gospel truth that, that's really true.

* Did you do all that stuff, Luchia, when you were a butch, like not wanting to be touched when you were in bed?
Oh yeah, yeah, yeah, you take it all over, yeah. All that shit . . .

* It must have made you quite unhappy, that?
Yeah, 'twas. I was as miserable as fuck. I used to end up like having a wank myself, you know. I'd go in the bathroom after a while, you know, and have a wank myself like, you know what I mean?

* I was going to ask you about the band too, Luchia. When did the band form up? When you got into music?
Well, when I was younger like, you know, we always had a family band and I used to sing in that. It was mainly country and western, and I always wanted to, when I grew up, to be in a band.

* Did you play any instrument?
No, I didn't. I used to sing. Then in the Women's Movement I was always thinking, Jeeze, it would be great if we could get our own band together. So then we started talking seriously about it

one night. We used to have parties at the Women's Centre – discos and that, and people brought their own records. We were talking one night about why did we always have to listen to shit? Why do we have to dance to this sort of shit? And we switched off the record player one night and started having a sing-song. Let's sing something, you know, boom boom, you know, that we can relate to. So what happened was we decided that we should have our own gig. All the people we said that had guitars and what have you or that could sing, do anything, fuck, anything at all, get along down to the Women's Centre on Sunday. So they did, everybody brought along different things, and we decided we'd have a bash at everything to see what everybody's potential was, or ability, and that's how we formed it.

* What was it called? The Northern Women's Rock Band?
No, not at the time, because we did a lot of practising and getting together and people were very shy and stuffy, you know?

* Yeah. How long did you take to get it together?
We were practising about nine months before the Edinburgh conference that was the first . . .

* Was yours the first women's band in England?
Yeah, first women's liberation band in England. Yeah, I think so. We're getting another one together now, by the way.

* What kind of band will it be?
Well, you see, I think as far as women and sexism in music is concerned, we've a long way to go, and I find this very hard to explain. You see, I don't think that we should lay trips on a women's band or make superstars out of them because I don't think we should be competing. I would love to see lots of women's bands playing women's music and not competing against each other.

* You want it to be on a much more informal basis, in other words?
Mmm, yes, but it's the comparing thing, you know what I mean, and, 'Oh they'd be better off if they had a different guitarist.' These are the sort of things, you know, the Northern Women's Rock Band try to break down.

* Should be like anyone could get up and join you?

Yeah, but you have to be very careful of the way you do that. You've got to practise that before you get up, otherwise you're going to be bamboozled on the stage. I think like, that you should put out some sort of a leaflet on the day like, come along if you want to rehearse with the band, you know, because that's got to be a bit together. Something like that, and let's bring out everybody's ability, you know, have the band of women backing them, and if someone can play the guitar, they can come up and do it as well, with the rest.

* And have the words of your songs available to people, too?
Yes, and people appreciating those words, you know. 'Cause the words to me is everything, do you know what I mean? I think it's what you're fucking saying that makes everything.

* And when everyone's into it, the music kind of sounds good.
Yeah, it just comes out, you know what I mean?

* It's a completely different concept from popular music now, you know, male popular music.
Well, this is – now you've hit the nail on the head. What I'm trying to say is, let's make our own thing, let's not try to live up to or be better than them.

* Real music and not imitation men's music.
Exactly, which I see as different, totally different.

* That sounds great.
But that's what the Northern Women's Rock Band has tried to put across anyway.

* Is there anything else you'd like to say or talk about?
I'd like to go back and say that, you know, although my mother is not in the Women's Movement, when she fucked off on her husband and nine months in the Women's Centre really fucking brought it home to her. She lived there for nine months and she's really changed.

* All the ideas are getting to her?
Yeah, I mean it was important for me that I changed, you know, the only thing in the world that I wished was that she'd change as well, and that we would sort of become close. I had a hang-up about her and she had a hang-up about me. The hang-up I had about her is that she never wanted me. The hang-up she had about me

was that she left my granny to rear me. Because I thought for her to have me was her downfall. Are you with it? I never forgave her and she always sort of had a thing about me. And since she came to the Women's Centre we talked and talked and different things and me and my mother are like sisters now. That's the only thing I wanted in my life for me and her, you know, to be the best of friends.

* She was a battered wife for twenty years. She's only forty-five now, isn't she?
She had me when she was fourteen. So she's really started . . .

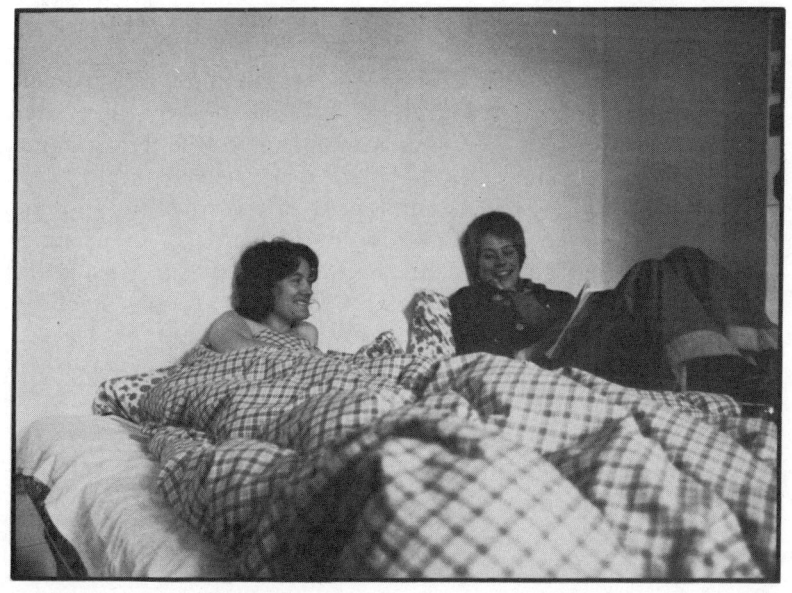

* So the man that she's married to isn't your father, though?
No.

* And at fourteen, she was put in a nursing home for two years and kept there forcibly?
Till I was two.

* How did she get out of there?
Well, it was come-for-adoption day, see, and they had me sitting up on the fucking rocking horse with lots of other kids, and she

sort of realized and she was looking at me. I was going up for adoption, and she went over and swiped me off the fucking horse and said, 'Don't fucking bother, I'll keep her, fuck it.' Because, you know, she wasn't allowed back in the house with me, so then it was either, you know, her keep me, or she could have gone out to work, you see, in these places. These nuns, you see, set things up for you. You know, where you can go and have your baby, and then you're a slave until your child is sixteen. By Jesus something like, or till you're old enough to fucking hang up your guns. So then she thought, Fuck it, so she kept me and went to work in this hospital and then my granny reared me.

* So you became friends again in the Manchester Women's Centre?

Yeah. She came down to me one night, you should have seen her. She let herself go and she looked like a woman of sixty. She never went outside the door. She was very unhappy. She was stinking with the dirt. She never bothered to make herself up or wash herself. That's the way she went after twenty years of it. Now she fucking decks herself out, I don't mean with make-up or anything. She cleans herself up, she's up every fucking morning, she's out every fucking night enjoying herself. When she was seventeen up till she was twenty-nine, she had a baby every fucking year. And the doctor over here sort of, you know, gave her that operation when she was twenty-nine.

* Seventeen to twenty-nine, that's twelve kids.

In fact I think she had thirteen altogether. She's got eight up there with her. They're nearly all married off now, there's three now and me.

* Good grief!

She was that poor, right? She never had fuck-all. She was that poor she had to bury one in a shoe box. You know, like when she had it, like, it was dead or it died. She had all of them at home in the fucking bed, you know, she got that used to having them. She used to have them herself and cut the cord and all and do it all herself, yeah.

* Of course she'd never use contraception?

That wasn't available at the time, sure. No, the pill wasn't available when she had children.

* And she'd be under a lot of pressure from her husband and the Church?
She was. She doesn't believe in all that fucking shit now.

* Have you talked about that?
Oh yeah, we talked about all that. She comes down, you know, and we go for a drink and maybe have a few bevvies and we talk a lot about . . .

* How does she get on with your dyke friends?
She loves them all. She thinks they're the best fucking crowd she's ever met. She loves every one of them. She fucking loves them all. She's always saying, 'Bring them all up, it doesn't fucking matter,' you know, she loves them all, which is amazing, you know, from what she's come from.

Debee Moskowitz

Debee Moskowitz is twenty-one. She was born in Brooklyn and grew up in Long Island, New York. At present she is studying communications in New Paltz.

* Are your family a real Jewish family?
As opposed to a fake one? [*Laughter.*]

* As opposed to just of Jewish origins?
Well, they are into the culture of it, but not the whole religious part of it, like going to the temple and stuff.

* You don't have the sabbath on Saturday and . . .
No, we just do it up for the big holidays, that's about all.

* And you go to bar mitzvahs and all that?
Used to, yeah, when I was younger and stuff – my brother got bar mitzvah'd, the whole . . .

* And they still get into that, do they – your parents?
Yeah, my mother keeps the house kosher as well, two separate sets of silverware, but we'll go out and eat something that's not kosher. It's not something you could follow along logical lines and say, 'That doesn't make sense.'

* Did you go to a Jewish school?
No, it was a public school – you know what a public school is in the States?

* High school.
Yeah, regular schools that the state provides and everybody goes to, and very few Jewish people go to Jewish schools.

* And what about after high school, what did you do then?
I went straight into college after that. It's called communication arts, the course. It covers more than just broadcasting. You could do art courses and include them as part of your communications studies.

* Are you career-orientated?

137

I don't see how I could be, 'cos I can't figure out how I could have a career and not compromise myself. I just don't know how I could do that – what I'm into it for now is to get as many technical skills and as much technical knowledge as possible, and then see where it leads from there, see if I could do things with women – video and/or film or radio or television whichever, just to get as much out of them, to use the equipment . . .

* What were you aware of first, were you aware of the Women's Movement or aware of lesbianism first?
The Women's Movement.

* When was that?
When I was about fifteen, it was pretty much through radio programmes that I first started getting into it – on this radio station in New York – and started listening to this women's programme when feminism was first really getting going and getting into the media, and gradually the woman that did that show came out as a lesbian, and I kind of grew somewhat with her, and was ready to come out for about a year before I did. I was with a lot of lesbians, but I didn't feel very good with them, they were putting a lot of pressure on me to come out and I wasn't meeting anybody that I felt was very receptive. They were also into a lot of man-hating and I wasn't, and as they were the only lesbians I knew, I figured, well, if these are what lesbians are then I must not be one.

* Were you attracted to women at this time, though?
Yeah, and also I was able to trace back other times when I felt that with other women – teachers, camp counsellors and things like that, but I hadn't really faced up to it, I was trying to struggle with why no men were attracted to me.

* Were you attracted to them?
No, not really, I went out on a few dates, but I never liked the guys who were attracted to me, so I didn't even count them, 'cos I didn't like them, and then suddenly I realized there weren't any men that I really wanted to go out with. There was one that I sort of liked, but that never happened with him, and that was about all. I never had a relationship with a man, the most I ever had was a few dates, and I never really enjoyed any of them and I didn't have any really close men friends until I came out and they've mostly been gay men.

* Did you ever have any sexual relationships with men?
No, the most it came down to was a goodnight kiss, and I was always trying to make sure that the door was between us or that my cheek was turned or something like that.

* Have you ever had that thing thrown up at you – well, how do you know that you prefer going to bed with a woman, when you've never been to bed with a man?
Yeah, I have.

* How do you deal with that, what do you feel about that?
I usually try and turn it around, like if it's a heterosexual person asking me that, I usually say, 'You wouldn't question a heterosexual person like that, you wouldn't doubt their heterosexuality by saying you have never slept with somebody of your own sex.' I think you can judge what you want to do. I know that if I'm not attracted to a man and don't feel turned on to him, I don't have to go through sex before I know that.

* Do you think lesbianism and feminism are always compatible? You know, necessarily so completely intertwined?
They are intertwined for me. I mean, I can't separate my politics from my emotional feelings and my – even my physical attractions. You know the kind of women on the cover of *Glamour* and *Vogue* and all those magazines, I don't find them attractive, I find them kind of strangely painted and I can somewhat objectively say, yes, by this culture's standards she has a pretty nose and pretty eyes and a pretty mouth, but I can't get turned on to women any more when I can't see – both elements of strength and gentleness, and that combination's what turns me on about women. But that is kind of along those same lines that your politics kind of have to colour the rest of your life, making you decide what appeals to you and what doesn't in all sorts of ways.

* Do you think the Women's Movement takes itself too seriously at times?
No, I think it's – no, not at all, I think it's very serious, I think there's a need for radically changing the whole culture and that's a very serious matter. It should be taken very seriously.

* Are you happy being a lesbian?
Yeah. It's sometimes hard to see.

* Why?
Because it's still – I still feel that we are at the very beginning of forming any kind of supportive community and I still see lots of women messing each other over and just behaving in really irresponsible ways. I'm sure I do it in certain ways just because we're not used to trusting each other and not used to really behaving in the ways that our politics or our philosophies say that we want to behave. We still screw up, we're bound to, but I'm still hopeful most of the time – and I still feel that there's no other way I want to live, and I want to move on with it and I think we will.

* Were you born a dyke, do you think, or was it environmental? Why do you think you are?
I can never answer that question. I think it's a combination of – I don't think you're born a dyke, I think it's more environmental – if you grow up wanting to be whole as a woman in this society, then you have to be a feminist because I just can't see how you could not be, and once you are a feminist it's almost impossible to have any kind of whole relationship with a man because there's all kinds of roles that you're all taught, and even if he's really cool, you know, other people lay trips on you and it's all so ingrained. That's the only way that I can see myself going really from a strong person, to a feminist to a lesbian, it's just a very logical progression.

* So in a way you think being a lesbian is a political action to put yourself outside the thing you are trying to destroy, which is the heterosexual life-style – the assumption that all women are there for men's pleasure and to bear their children?
Yeah, they're very much intertwined with each other, there's really very little separating the two for me, my politics from my attractions or my life-style or any of those things.

* Can you remember when you were a child, comparing yourself to the boys around you that you grew up with?
Yeah, I did it, and other people did it, because I was always playing sports with them and stuff, and there'd be sometimes very uncomfortable comparisons – I remember one time when I was at summer camp I was called Amazon and it freaked me out, I couldn't handle it, I was very upset about it . . .

* What did you think it meant, that it upset you?

I guess it meant to me that I wasn't attractive to men and I needed to be because I needed their approval, because it meant I wouldn't have a boy-friend, it meant I wouldn't have a husband, it meant no one would ever love me, I didn't think that I'd ever . . . that I could just live with women, when I was eleven I didn't think that out or anything, I thought I was going to be alone and I was, you know, afraid, but I didn't stop . . .

* What do you think Amazon means now?
I think – I think it means pretty much the same thing that I thought it meant then, but I'm not afraid of it any more.

* What, unattractive to men?
Well, I think an Amazon is probably somebody who men would be afraid of, because I think that most men need to see women weak in order to appreciate them; you know, they love you best when you're crying and they want to take care of you, that kind of thing, but I don't think that there are too many men that love strong women, whole women, and I don't think too many men can handle whole, strong, healthy women.

* What is your feeling about separatists, are you a separatist?
No, I'm not a separatist.

* What does it mean to you? It's a word that's bandied about a lot, isn't it?
Yeah. I have friends who are separatists, they're into buying land and moving off and having absolute minimal contact with men or the male culture, and there's a part of me that obviously feels that and sympathizes with that, but I think now that I couldn't move off into one of those communes because I feel like I'd get more cut off than I want to right now. I'm not into dealing with men all the time and confronting them and all that, but I'm not into cutting myself off completely either. What's happening I think in New York is that the separatists are condemning the women that they think are straight because they are still living in cities or dealing with men on any kind of terms, and those women are condemning the separatists because they're splitting themselves off, and I think that both functions are necessary because the separatists create a space where women can go and the other women create a certain contact which is necessary for survival. I've thought sometimes about an ideal little island where there's this women's culture, and I think if there was one it wouldn't be long before some government, probably the US government, would come along and drop a little bomb on the island, you know, and that's why I think that for our survival it's necessary to stay in cultural contact with society.

* Do you see separatist communities as a refuge so that women can remove themselves from society for a while and sort themselves out?
Yeah.

* If you were a separatist, for instance, in a separatist commune, and women were continually coming in from the outside and staying for a while then leaving, don't you think that you would be in touch?
Yeah, which is why I think it's so important. I mean ideally that's how it should work, that those women could give their contribution by creating the space and the women that are in the male culture could give their contribution. What tends to happen, or what's happening now, is that the two groups are not accepting each other as giving viable contributions – they're putting each other down and trying to decide who's superior and who's the better feminist,

and that's where the danger comes in, 'cos we cut each other off and the Women's Movement is getting so splintered that women are doing each other in – for example, what's happening in the States with all those trials, where women who used to be involved with the Weathermen are being done in by lesbian feminists who are saying, 'Well, they were involved with men, so they're no good'; and also doing in men, that shouldn't be cast off either.

* You mean men from the radical left?
Not necessarily from the radical left, but men who have an idea of sexual politics and want to change that structure too. I mean, that's no good either along the same lines – to see men as the enemy because of their physiology instead of finding out what they are about.

* So you don't hate men?
Not categorically, no. Most of them I find I don't have much to say to, but there are still the rare few that I want to stay open to talking with.

* What are your feelings about children? Would you like to have a child yourself?
Yeah, I really like children a lot, I like being around them, and I'd like to be involved with raising them with other women. I could never do it alone or with one other woman, I wouldn't want to, I would want it to be with more people than that. I think that a lot of the problem with the way that we are brought up is this whole strange relationship that children and parents have, where the children are the property of the parents, and that's a very dangerous and a very unhealthy thing for anybody. Children shouldn't be older people's property any more than women should be the property of men.

* How old were you, Debee, when you had your first sexual experience with a woman?
Nineteen.

* Were you in love with her?
Yes, it went on for about – well, I like to think that it's still going on – well that's one of my goals – to not end relationships with lovers because we've stopped being lovers and to continue with what we have because – the whole thing of being with women and loving

them is that I'll be friends with them first and the friendship will be really the most important thing and making love will be an extension of that – my attraction to them and my love for them – that's something I'm still very much struggling with. I met that woman in a feminist class and we got friendly and then we started seeing each other, and the understanding was that we'd see other people throughout, but I really wasn't – she was – and I really wasn't handling that all that well – I was also feeling a lot of jealousy, and I wasn't able to sort out what it was all about. From the very beginning she made it very clear that she was seeing other people and she

wanted to continue doing so. OK, my reaction was that this was fine, but then dealing with it when it was happening was a whole other story.

* Jealousy?

Yes – and I had a lot of trouble with that – and I think that part of the problem was that the friendship base wasn't strong enough with us. I haven't given up on that yet – I still want to be friends with her and I still love her. I think it's different with Jane – we're really good friends, and that is the strength of our relationship, our friendship and our trust.

* Are you into dyke couple relationships – do you approve of them?
No – well – to an extent I find it necessary for myself to have one person who's the primary relationship in my life, but I guess that's because I'm afraid of being alone – if there was the ideal women's community that I'm struggling towards I think I wouldn't have that fear, I'd know that when one thing stopped there'd be other women around to support me, but we're kind of between worlds now – we're struggling towards those ideals but still living with all that thing that we've been brought up in where people have to be in a couple because you have to be in a nuclear family and you have to deny your attractions for other people because you'll threaten that structure, and threatening the nuclear family threatens the whole rest of the structure.

* Have you ever been into one-night stands – you know, casual sexual encounters?
I'm not quite sure what that means – I've never met a woman and then just gone right off and slept with her after meeting her, like at a bar or something like that.

* What are the elements that go to make up someone – a woman – who sexually attracts you, then?
Well, I think basically what I summed up before in saying that I'm very attracted to women that are strong and soft at the same time, that allow what we've learned to call masculine and feminine sides of themselves through and accept their weaknesses and strengths as positive, because I think that what started to happen in the beginning with feminism was that we started hating ourselves and hating women, hating femininity, and we rejected it all; and I think that women are just starting to turn back and appreciate women, appreciate women's culture, appreciate women's art, you know, and realize its beauty; and you can have that gentleness and strength.

* Why do you love women? That's my favourite question.
Because I think again, that whole thing – I think that women are in tune with their gentleness and can give me that kind of support that . . . I think men are more freaked out about their gentleness

145

than women are about their strength, so it's easier to get to that strength, and they can combine that gentleness and strength, and I think that they are very – the women that I love are . . .

* Why do you like making love with women?
I like women's bodies, I like their softness, I like being held in the way that women hold me, and I like also the other side of it, the excitement that we generate in each other when we make love.

* Were you frightened the first time?
Yeah, it took a long time, well, also the thing that was odd about me was that I'd never, I mean all I had done was those good-night kisses with a man, so it wasn't just my first woman, it was my first sexual relationship, and it took a while before . . . I thought my body wasn't too nice, I didn't want to show my body, and it took a while before we'd worked up – all those years that everybody goes through in their teens working up step by step, making out and then petting and then going on to sleeping with each other, and I was doing that all in one. It was like a crash course or something.

* What were you frightened about – you didn't know what to do and all that one?
No, no, I wasn't frightened that I didn't know what to do. I was afraid that she would think that I was ugly, and 'cos I thought that I was ugly . . . and I'm still not quite over that you know, I'm still not into thinking that I'm all wonderful and OK and beautiful. I can say that to other women, and say, 'You're OK and really beautiful and accept yourself,' but I'm not quite there myself, you know. So it took a while building up with us, and she was very, very beautiful, very sensitive, and went just as slowly as I needed to go, which I don't think a man might have done. He would have probably got into a thing about how I was leading him on and teasing him and that whole number, and she was very receptive and very gentle with me and waiting while I got through that whole thing.

* And you were sort of freaking out, were you, at first?
No, because she wasn't pushing me. That's why that happened with that bunch of lesbians that I knew at first – they were saying, 'Well, what are you? Are you a dyke?' and I felt very pressured and I felt I wasn't given the space to grow into it, the way I needed,

and I see that still happening. Women that I know do that to other women that haven't committed themselves to calling themselves lesbians, and won't give them . . . other dykes often won't give them the space to grow into what they need to grow into, in this space and time that they need to grow into it, and I had that; I was very lucky to have that and I really needed it.

* What about now, would you sleep with a man now, ever?
I mean I feel certain pressures like we were talking about before. I've never slept with a man, so, you know, I feel there is still a slight residual pressure, particularly when I talk it out with my mother. She thinks that – she'll say sometimes, 'Well, you're scared,' and things, and I don't think it's that I'm scared, it's that I'm not inclined to. I don't think it's possible to have a healthy heterosexual relationship in a sexist society. So unless sexism is totally eradicated in my lifetime (which I find highly unlikely, even in my most optimistic moments), it would be really stupid for me to enter a handicapped relationship with a man when I can be having such beautiful, strong, positive ones with women.

* The idea doesn't excite you?
No, it doesn't excite me right now, no, I'm having a really nice time with women. [*Laughter.*]

* (J) Hardly any men know how to kiss properly, let alone how to fuck properly, so you're not missing out on anything, I can tell you that for sure from long experience.

* (A) What is your idea of a perfect lesbian relationship?
Well, I think that it's an open one, yeah, kind of what we were talking about before – being open and being supportive of women who aren't your lover, and ideally that's very important for me to be involved with and sensitive to my friends and treat them with the importance they deserve and not just go back and take care of me and this one woman. I mean it's not what a whole dyke community is about, is it?

* When you first found out about lesbians, how did you think they did it?
I think from the first time I thought about it I knew how it would be. When I first made love with Rosa it was – this flash of – yeah, this is how I knew it would be.

* How did you think you would make love with a woman?

It was always very gentle, and it was always pretty much what I'm doing now with women, because I didn't have that experience with men where it's like him trying to get you and you trying to fight him off. It was never like that, 'cos it's not what I think natural sex is about. That's what sex has become between men and women because, you know, women have all this to protect about their reputation and all this kind of thing about not screwing until you're married and stuff, so that wouldn't happen between women because – obviously it wouldn't happen . . . I was thinking about if I was going to have my parents read this book at some point.

* How do you feel about that?

I'm trying to go as slowly with them as I feel they need to go, and, you know, which is hard because sometimes . . . it's that whole thing of communicating with people you know, you have this dual thing you want on the one hand to express what you're feeling, and on the other hand you want to say as much as will not turn them off, 'cos you want to get the message across first, or I want to with them, that's why I waited a long time before I came out to my mother and did it when I thought she'd be ready for it – and still don't tell her all that I think, all the thoughts that I have on women and men. I go as slowly as I feel she can handle it.

* Well, did you tell them you were going to be in this book?

Well, eventually I'm sure I will. I mean, it's moving, our talking about it, and we're getting further with it and I think it will come to that point, I hope it will. I'm trying to talk with her about her feelings with it, and her reservations, and consider her and the whole thing and me. When I go down there, if they ask me what I've been doing in London, for instance, what I've been doing is mostly being with women, being with dykes and, you know, spending time with them and having relationships. [*Laughter.*]

Glossary

Arena Three lesbian magazine, forerunner to *Sappho* magazine.

Butch and femme (role-playing) lesbians who imitate male and female heterosexual roles in their lifestyle, speech and dress.

CHE Campaign for Homosexual Equality; has groups which meet all over the country.

Closet (in the closet, out of the closet, closet lesbian) refers to lesbians who hide their sexuality.

Coming out (coming out of the closet, q.v.) being open about your sexuality.

Crown and Woolpack a pub in Islington where women-only discos were held for a time.

Diesel a very butch (mannish) lesbian.

Dyke lesbian.

Femø a small Danish island where an international women's summer camp is held every year.

Gay homosexual (male or female).

Gay News fortnightly paper for homosexuals.

Gateways (the Gates) probably the oldest lesbian club in the country, in Bramerton Street, Chelsea. It's for members only and is open every night till 11.

Hampstead Ponds *see* Women's pool.

Parthenogenesis natural reproduction without sexual intercourse.

Sappho lesbian magazine and group which holds weekly meetings on Tuesdays at the Chepstow pub, Chepstow Place, London W2.

SCUM Manifesto revolutionary book on sexism by Valerie Solanas, published by Olympia Press.

Separatists feminist women who avoid all contact with men.

Straight heterosexual when referring to sexual orientation; conservative, conventional when referring to lifestyle.

Women's pool an open-air swimming pool on Hampstead Heath for women only.

Workshop, the Women's Information and Newsletter Service (formerly Women's Liberation Workshop), Central London Women's Centre and Bookshop, Earlham Street, London WC1. It is now called A Woman's Place.